Archbishop Derek Worlock

GIVE ME YOUR HAND

Jesus spoke to Thomas, '... Give me
your hand; put it into my side. Doubt
no longer but believe.'

John 20:27

 St Paul Publications

8486

ST PAUL PUBLICATIONS
SLOUGH SL3 6BT ENGLAND

Copyright © St Paul Publications 1977
First published April 1977
Printed by the Society of St Paul, Slough
ISBN 0 85439 133 9

for
PATRICK KEEGAN
who has helped so many
to understand and love
the Church

CONTENTS

INTRODUCTION

Journalists are always looking for a water-shed in a man's life: a turning-point, a moment of decision. For some people such happenings are deliberate, sought after, even planned. More commonly these moments are long drawn out, scarcely identifiable until they have passed. They are situations insufficiently appreciated at the time but looked back upon with wonder.

Such was my involvement in the Second Vatican Council. Eighteen years have passed since on 25th January 1959 a newspaperman telephoned me to say "Pope John's done it again. He's called an ecumenical Council. Your comments, please". All I could remember from my theological training was my professor's opinion that with the coming of the dogma of infallibility there would never need to be another Council. Evidently I still had much to learn.

By God's mercy I was to be involved in the Second Vatican Council at every stage: from its preparatory commissions to my work as a consultant or *peritus* throughout the Council itself. In the final session I was appointed a bishop and so had to cast my vote on some of the decrees which in a very small measure I had helped to prepare. Later I was to serve on a post-Conciliar commission which led to ten years with the Holy See's Laity Council. It was perhaps the longest and most thorough-going in-service training to which anyone might be submitted after twenty years of priesthood.

As a newly-appointed bishop at the end of the Council I was not unnaturally asked by the priests and people of my diocese what they were to expect and where my priorities would lie. With a somewhat superficial over-statement I replied "We shall try to do the lot. Neither you nor I will pick and choose. We will follow each decree and all subsequent implementing legislation. In a time of change

1

to 'stay with Peter' is the best touchstone of orthodoxy".

If Pope John did not, as is often alleged, realise what forces he was releasing when he summoned the Second Vatican Council, I certainly had no idea of the full measure required by that first undertaking I gave. Yet it has been a great strength. Over the years we have seen the new relationships and responsibilities of the post-Conciliar Church develop. We have seen the greater emergence of the whole of the people of God. All are affected by the Church's call for renewal for "I know that what God does, he does consistently" (Eccles 3:14).

This consistent development has meant many meetings and the creation of many new structures. Both "meetings" and "structures" have become to some extent dirty words nowadays, yet both have been necessary in a period when all have had to learn and some means of sharing have had to be devised. It has also meant and still means many speeches: proclaiming God's word in the whole process of renewal. Being consistent has meant that these principles of a renewed faith and of Gospel-living must be applied to each ministry and to each aspect of the Church's mission in a constantly changing society.

Often it has meant breaking new ground. When some experience has been gained or a telling address has been delivered to good effect, people say all too simply "Why doesn't he write it all down?" This book is an attempt to meet that request. This is not to pretend that we have found all the answers or indeed that some of the first answers are still the right ones. But it does represent a willingness to examine the consequences of the Church's new understanding of her nature and task in today's world. It represents a response to the call expressed by Pope Paul at the beginning of the Council's second session, soon after his coming to the papacy:

> "This self-awareness of the Church is clarified by faithful adherence to the words and thoughts of Christ, by respectful attention to the teaching of ecclesiastical

tradition and by docility to the interior illumination of the Holy Spirit, who seems to be requiring of the Church today to do all that she can to make known what she really is".

These words were prophetic. Often in the last years, when we have run into difficulties and opposition, the only explanation that could be offered has been "They have not understood what the Church is all about". This book is an attempt to say very simply what the Church is all about. It tries to suggest how at various levels clergy, religious and laity can share in the life and ministry of a Church renewed. It is not a complete compendium of pastoral theology but it contains no recommendation that has not been tried. Its chapters are drawn from thoughts expressed over the years on a variety of occasions. For their great help in bringing all the material together in this book I am deeply grateful to my friends Father Nicholas France, Sister Maria Hegarty and Mrs Jane Nixon who typify those who have inspired much of the thoughts here presented.

The Englishman's approach is said to be pragmatic. It need be no worse for this. In finding his way forward he can often progress only by stages and in the light of experience gained. In Christian renewal, because of the sacred nature of his mission, faith is required as well as courage. I am always heartened by the story of Pope John who, after marvelling at the skill of astrologers, remarked that for himself he was content, like Abraham, to go forward one step at a time into the darkness but with his hand in that of the Lord.

Surely it was in the same spirit that the faith of the apostle St Thomas was praised by the Saviour to whom he responded when he heard the words "Give me your hand".

+ DEREK WORLOCK
Archbishop of Liverpool

January 1977

VATICAN II: THE AFTERMATH

In the end is my beginning. So it was with the Second Vatican Council and with me. Midway through the final session in 1965 I was appointed a bishop. Although I could not receive episcopal ordination until I might return to England when the Council was over, I was enabled as a bishop-elect to cast my vote for the Decree on the Lay Apostolate and the Pastoral Constitution on The Church in the Modern World which had occupied so much of my time during the previous years when I was attached as a *peritus* (expert or adviser) to the Council. My change in status was marked by my compulsory removal from the "periti-box" in St Peter's where I had spent so much time with the other experts and banished to a lofty tribune, reserved for bishops but where — perhaps significantly — I could see and hear notably less than before.

The last stages of the Council occupied us until 8th December. The closing ceremony, at which I was told I might legitimately wear a bishop's skull-cap for the first time, took place in the Piazza outside St Peter's but was in fact the third scene of the final act. On 4th December in an unprecedented inter-denominational liturgy of the Word, held in St Paul's Basilica, Pope Paul had shown the way ahead to his brother bishops. Standing simply in front of an ordinary straight-back chair, (allegedly rushed into the basilica to replace the customary magnificent throne of majestic proportions), the Holy Father had pointed out that this great Council had issued not anathemas but invitations. "May this ray of divine light", he said, "cause us all to recognise the blessed door of truth".

Three days later it was the turn of the Orthodox. In the final public session in St Peter's on 7th December, a joint declaration was read out, signed by Pope Paul and the Orthodox Patriarch of Constantinople. It was a statement not only burying the mutual excommunications of the past but serving as an invitation to the entire Christian world to seek the ultimate unity for which Christ prayed the night before he died.

Then out in the Piazza, on 8th December 1965, a whole series of Conciliar messages were read out: once again invitations to all categories of the human family to receive and respond to the decrees and initiatives of the Council. The various formalities complete, Pope Paul dismissed the assembly with a final blessing: "*Ite in pace* — go in peace". "My peace I leave with you, my peace I give unto you, but not as the world gives it". Pope Paul had quoted those words from St John's gospel in his closing address, emphasising that this greeting was not strictly a farewell but the establishment of a new relationship into which Christ himself entered: Christ working in and through the framework of human relationships. This was to be an outstanding characteristic of the renewed Church-community.

It is good that, before we begin to examine the pastoral opportunities that confront the Church today, we should remember that sunny but chill morning when the Council ended and the post-Conciliar age began. Experiences will have differed and my skull-cap, donned for the first time that December day, has known both the heat of the day and the chill winds of reaction. When sometimes the storm has broken, and both zeal and truth have been misrepresented, we have learned, my skull-cap and I, to "keep our cool".

It was on the feast of St Thomas the Apostle that I

6

was "consecrated", as we then called episcopal ordination. Archbishop Thomas Roberts sent me a telegram saying rather ambiguously "May the spirit of St Thomas uphold you". Not altogether fairly St Thomas, who made that wonderful profession of faith "My Lord and My God", is still known to most as doubting Thomas. But in 1965 we had all to learn the meaning of "The Questioning Church". I think I had already realised that to be a bishop in the post-Vatican II era was going to be very different from being the kind of bishop who had gone before. This was no criticism of my predecessors but the realisation that society was changing at an unprecedented rate and that the Church, in her structures at least and in the manner of her ministry, would inevitably be affected by the society in which she was situated and which she must endeavour to serve.

In this I was not assuming the mantle of a prophet: I merely was trying to apply the two key doctrines which were emerging from the long Conciliar debate, then gradually taking shape in decrees. I refer to collegiality and co-responsibility. This theological jargon requires explanation. Briefly, collegiality means that the members of the college of bishops (as successors of the apostles), in union with the Pope (as successor of Peter and bishop of Rome), whilst each exercises jurisdiction over his own diocese, also share solicitude for the whole universal Church. Co-responsibility, on the other hand, means that all the members of the Church, each according to his ministry and role in life, share responsibility for the mission entrusted by Christ to his followers: to bring the light of the Gospel to the world.

What effect have these two factors — collegiality and co-responsibility — had upon my being a bishop? It will probably be easier if the second is considered first: that is the kind of world in which we live.

Co-responsibility in the life and mission of the Church has come at a time when society at large is talking about participation. It is more than just consultation. It is sharing in the task of the Church, each in accord with his ministry,

7

vocation, role, and in the sphere in which the individual has his whole being. It means an end to "churchiness" and "outside-churchiness", an end to clericalism and anti-clericalism, an end to Sunday-suit religion and weekday secularism.

It means commitment to the cause of Christ at home, at work, in church: the realisation that the Church is people. The layman endeavouring to work out his Christian principles in the factory, the father in his office, the mother out shopping for her family, the nurse changing dressings in the hospital, the boy learning at school, all these are just as much the Church as the priest preaching and baptising, the nun spending long hours in prayer in her chapel. Not only are they *being* the Church, they also share responsibility for worshipping God and loving and serving their neighbour, whoever that is.

The task of a bishop in regard to all these people is first of all to preach, to teach, to inspire by word and by personal example in a way that they can understand, see, hear and respond to. He must try to practise what he preaches if his words are to be in any sense credible. He must try to direct and coordinate their endeavours for the greater glory of God and for the more effective character of their witness.

This has meant of course that nearly all diocesan and parish structures have had to be re-shaped. Whilst the administration and structural side of what is called nowadays the "institution" has to be preserved or improved, renewal cannot be a mere take-over by one body or caste from another. It is an intensification of the desire to evangelise — and this by as many as possible: not a 1st XI of clerics and a sizeable supporters' club turning out once a week, but whole-time apostles integrated in the life of the Church and into society as it really is. All this has to be carried out against a background of steadily-spreading secularisation: the inculcation of enthusiasm and zeal amidst a general setting of Western-world apathy. This cannot be done from a desk. The proclaimer must go out where he can be seen and heard and can teach and inspire.

It probably seems a little phoney when I hesitate on being asked: "What do you do with your leisure time?" — which is usually supplementary to "I suppose you are kept fairly busy at Christmas". Most bishops have large dioceses to cover — the Cathedral or Bishop's House is only a base. On most days in a year a bishop must be on the move — visiting parishes, schools and all manner of groups and institutions. Frequently he must meet with his priests to consult with them. There is also a deal to be done with civic authorities, professional bodies, assemblies of various kinds, even Pop Festivals: trying to give witness, wherever Christ would have gone. There are ecumenical works with other Christians and national commitments with the Bishops' Conference and the commissions which work in the name of the bishops.

Is all this being a bishop today? That takes me to the second factor in the life of the Church today: collegiality. This is sharing some measure of responsibility and concern for the whole Church throughout the world. For some this is a reality in that soon after the Vatican Council the Holy See began to appoint a few bishops from dioceses outside Rome to share in this work of central government in the various departments of the Church.

There had been all kinds of requests to internationalise the Curia and some of us have been the sacrificial offerings made to the universal Church. It involves one in a great deal of correspondence and several visits to Rome each year.

There, all wired up with microphones, head-phones and simultaneous translation, in the Laity Council, for example, some 15 laity and 4 bishops (an Asian, an African, a Latin American and myself for Europe) struggled through long hours to help in the promotion of lay activity throughout the world and to sort out problems, many of them arising from national and political situations.

Is this being a post-Vatican II bishop? I believe it is.

I am a bishop when working in my diocese or outside. I feel that I am a part of the apostolic work overseas of my priests and people. Sometimes I get a little weary, like St Paul, "in journeying often". Malcolm Muggeridge once wrote a book about St Paul and called it *Envoy Extraordinary*. As a bishop, exercising what is called ordinary jurisdiction over my diocese — the jurisdiction which comes from office — I am also an envoy sent in the name of Christ and of that diocese to the whole Church. It may not be just what I anticipated when I stood outside St Peter's at the end of the Council. But it explains why I have sometimes felt justified in calling myself "Envoy-Ordinary". That is what the post-Conciliar bishop has to try to be.

STRUCTURES AND RELATIONSHIPS
IN THE POST-CONCILIAR CHURCH

In September 1965 the bishops of the Catholic Church, major religious superiors, the *periti*, the religious correspondents of the world's press and other members of the Conciliar circus gathered in Rome for what newspapermen had already dubbed "the fourth and final session" of the Second Vatican Council. Possibly because the previous session had ended in a somewhat querulous fashion, with the walk-out of three North American Cardinals frustrated at the postponement of a vote on religious liberty, it was generally accepted that this new session of the Second Vatican Council was to be in some way a test. "A test of sincerity" was one suggestion. Another newspaper, trying hard to get with it, came out with "a test of the Church's unflappability". But I remember best of all the remark made to me at that time by the English lay editor. Whilst we struggled to reacclimatise ourselves to several yards of spaghetti, Pat Keegan remarked with customary frankness: "The whole issue is whether the Council is able to show the world the face of Christ".

The idea of showing the face of Christ to the world was not a new one. If it was to the front of our minds at the end of the Council, it had also been placed before us by the stalwart Pope John at the opening ceremony in

11

October 1962: "Obeying the will of Christ, who delivered himself to death 'that he might present to himself the Church, not having spot or wrinkle but that she may be holy and without blemish', we as pastors devote all our energies and thoughts to the renewal of ourselves and the flocks committed to us, so that there may radiate before all men the loveable features of Jesus Christ, who shines in our hearts 'that God's splendour may be revealed' ".

Structures and relationships within the Church may seem at first to have little direct connection with the face of Christ. Yet time has shewn that these have been matters requiring our urgent attention if the Church of Christ is conscientiously to set about her task of portraying the charity and mercy of Christ to the world. In the past the Church has been known not only for her holiness but also for the unity and sense of security which have resulted from the teaching authority given to her by Christ and from the discipline (not always a fearsome thing) which has marked the exercise and acceptance of that authority. This is not to say that in the past blind obedience has been one of the marks of the Church. But it was clearly stated by the Second Vatican Council that in the Church there is no room for inequality and that responsibility for her mission is shared by all the baptised. It follows from this that the relationship between bishops, priests and laity is to be seen in a different light from that in which we once saw an hierarchically-structured Church resembling an ecclesiastical pyramid with, as Bishop McGrath of Panama once remarked, the laity running around like little acolytes at the base.

It is often said that *Lumen Gentium,* the Constitution on the Church, is the cornerstone of Conciliar teaching. Herein is contained the whole idea of a pilgrim Church, the people of God, "made one with the unity of the Father, the Son, and the Holy Spirit". Here we see the basic presentation of one Church, with one mission and a united voice. On this is built all the rest of the Conciliar teaching of the mission of all baptised persons to the entire human

12

race: "So it is that this messianic people, although it does not actually include all men, and may more than once look like a small flock, is nonetheless a lasting and sure seat of unity, hope, and salvation for the whole human race. Established by Christ as a fellowship of life, charity and truth, it is also used by him as an instrument for the redemption of all, and is sent forth into the whole world as the light of the world and the salt of the earth" (*Lumen Gentium,* 9).

If the Council emphasises the unity of the Church (God's family) and of her mission (the task entrusted by God to his family), it follows that stress must also be laid upon the sharing of responsibilities amongst the members of that family: bishops, priests, religious and laymen with differing roles but all with responsibilities. St Paul wrote: "You are all one in Christ Jesus". The Council reminds us: "Not all walk the same path in the Church but all are called to holiness. Priests and the rest of the faithful are closely related. The priests must serve each other and the rest of the faithful. The faithful must work with the clergy. Thus in his own way each witnesses to the unity that exists in Christ's Body" (*Lumen Gentium,* 32).

One uses the distinct words "structures" and "relationships". Yet within the Church these concepts are inter-related. There is an hierarchical structure in the Church, but it is unique in that the relationship between "superior" and "subject" must be fraternal for we are all brethren of Christ. The fact that it is Christ's Church demands that the structure is based on a relationship reaching out from brother to brother rather than a cold channel of communication through which commands are passed from head to foot. People are apt to identify an institution with an hierarchical structure, based on different roles within the Church, with institutionalism which means that the cold channel of communication has become frozen in such a way that leakage and rust will result. But the two are not the same. An institution, precisely because Christ instituted a Church, and structure, which is necessary for the preserva-

13

tion and development of truth, there must be. They are in any case needed for the good order in which the mission entrusted to all Christians must be carried out. But this is a relationship of love and service. The Church is made up of a people to whom God communicates himself in love. She is a community which seeks to penetrate more deeply into the mystery of Christ who dwells within her. Love and service lie at the very heart of the Church's authority and structure.

In our attempts to show the face of Christ to the world we look to the example of Christ to whom each one of us, no matter what his station in the Church, is subject. His humility, his obedience, his patience and his love must be our model. At the beginning of the third chapter of *Lumen Gentium*, on the hierarchical structure of the Church, we read: "For the nurturing and constant growth of the people of God, Christ the Lord instituted in his Church a variety of ministries, which work for the good of the whole body. For those ministers who are endowed with sacred power are servants of their brethren, so that all who are of the people of God, and therefore enjoy a true Christian dignity, can work toward a common goal freely and in an orderly way, and arrive at salvation" (*Lumen Gentium*, 18).

To help us to understand some of the problems of relationship within the Church at this time, we should do well to see what the Council has to say about the different roles of the bishop, the priest, the religious and the layman. I make no apology for such protracted use of quotations. It is not just that I seek the authority of the Church in Council, for what I am trying to say. Having spent so many years in Rome, engaged in work on pre-Conciliar, Conciliar and post-Conciliar documentation, I know the futility of trying to improve upon a task which has been well done.

What is a bishop's job? We are told in *Lumen Gentium* that "Among the principal duties of bishops, the preaching of the Gospel occupies an eminent place. For bishops are preachers of the faith who lead new disciples to Christ. They are authentic teachers, endowed with the authority of Christ, who preach to the people committed to them the faith they must live and put into practice" (*Lumen Gentium*, 25). The same theme is taken up in *Christus Dominus*, the Decree on the Bishops' Pastoral Office. In article 13 we are reminded that "The bishops should present Christian doctrine in a manner adapted to the needs of the times, that is to say, in a manner corresponding to the difficulties and problems by which people are most vexatiously burdened and troubled".

Secondary to his task of preaching the word of God lies the bishop's duty to develop the right relationships between himself, his priests and people: "Bishops govern the particular churches entrusted to them by their counsel, exhortations and example, as well as by their authority and sacred power" (*Lumen Gentium*, 27). They are referred to as good shepherds, a theme which is taken up in *Christus Dominus*: "In exercising his office of father and pastor, a bishop should stand in the midst of his people as one who serves. Let him be a good shepherd who knows his sheep and whose sheep know him. Let him be a true father who excels in the spirit of love and solicitude for all and to whose divinely conferred authority all gratefully submit themselves" (*Christus Dominus*, 16).

Now what is the job of the priest? There are many who are dissatisfied with the Council's document on the ministry and life of priests. It is argued that it took one Vatican Council to deal with the papacy and a second to deal with the episcopate: it will take a third to deal with the priesthood. This is not an argument which I would readily accept because to me the glory of the Second Vatican Council is its treatment of the Church. In the document on the Church, as also in the document on the pastoral care of dioceses, will be found much to emphasise the essential role of the priest in the life and mission of the Church. It is stressed that priests constitute one priesthood with their bishop and in a certain sense they make him present in the individual local congregations of the faithful. "As they sanctify and govern under the bishop's authority that part of the Lord's flock entrusted to them, they make the universal Church visible in their own locality and lend prayerful assistance to the building up of the whole Body of Christ" (*Lumen Gentium*, 28). They too are to preach the word of God. They too are to administer the sacraments and to make Christ present sacramentally in the community to which they minister. They are to strive to be a sign of leadership to God's people and to help form those entrusted to them into those "outward-looking worshipping communities with a Christian social purpose" — which is as near to a definition of a parish as I have been able to find.

The job of a religious? Once again we may look at the document on the Church: "Religious should carefully consider that through them, to believers and non-believers alike, the Church truly wishes to give an increasingly clearer revelation of Christ. Through them Christ should be shown contemplating on the mountain, announcing God's Kingdom to the multitude, healing the sick and the maimed, turning sinners to wholesome fruit, blessing children, doing good to all, and always obeying the will of the Father who sent him . . . Even though in some instances they do not directly mingle with their contemporaries, yet in a more profound sense these same religious are united with them in the heart of Christ and cooperate with them spiritually. In this way the work of building up the earthly city can always have its foundation in the Lord and can tend towards him. Otherwise, those who build the city will perhaps have laboured in vain" (*Lumen Gentium*, 6). Who shall say after that profound and beautiful piece of Conciliar writing, the religious has no place in the post-Conciliar Church, dedicated as it is to the service of mankind?

Lastly, what is the job of the layman? You may remember all the difficulties experienced by the Fathers of the Council in defining a layman. On the first occasion when this task came before them, they devoted nearly ten days to discussing what bishops thought laymen did. Once the full consideration of the Church had taken place, the layman's role was secure. Inevitably some part of the definition must be negative: "all the faithful except those in Holy Orders and those in the state of religious life, specially approved by the Church". Even this was better than the thirteenth century idea that the laity were those weak-kneed characters who could not undertake the rigours of the priesthood. Yet the positive approach was shared too: "Through baptism the faithful are made one body with Christ and make up the people of God. The faithful share Christ's role of priest, prophet and king and carry out the mission of God's people in the Church and in the world" (*Lumen Gentium*, 31).

Here one sees the importance of the appreciation that the layman's apostolate, "sharing in the salvific mission of the Church", can lie in secular things. "By their special vocation, the laity seek the Kingdom of God by engaging in temporal affairs ... by the disseminating of a life resplendent in faith, hope and charity, they make Christ known to others" (*Ibid.*). Indeed his special task is seen to be to make the Church present in those fields of human activity where he alone can penetrate effectively. Shown now his responsibilities as a baptised member of the Church, the layman has his full part to play in spiritual things as well as in the temporal order, in the worship of the Church as well as in his domestic and his professional life. But let us not be carried away into speaking of this as "the age of the layman". It is not the age of the layman. It is the age of the Church.

We have seen the different roles of different members of the Church. How can we ensure that the relationship between these different members is such that the work of the whole Church may redound to God's glory? What structure is needed to ensure the effective coordination of the work of the people of God, as individuals or as members of those parochial and diocesan communities which make up the Church?

So far as the relationship between bishop and priests is concerned, we can do no better than quote from the

17

Council's Decree on the Ministry and Life of Priests: "Therefore, on account of this communion in the same priesthood and ministry, the bishop should regard priests as his brethren and friends. As far as in him lies, he should have at heart the material and especially the spiritual welfare of his priests. For above all, upon the bishop rests the heavy responsibility for the sanctity of his priests. Hence, he should exercise the greatest care on behalf of the continual formation of his priests. He should gladly listen to them, indeed, consult them, and have discussions with them about those matters which concern the necessities of pastoral work and the welfare of the diocese" (*Christus Dominus*, 7).

It is delicate to speak in great detail on this point. Whereas positively we must uphold the whole notion of brotherhood between bishop and priests, we must face it that in practical terms the prime obstacle to this brotherhood is the "us and them" mentality. Once one tries to elaborate this theme, one immediately starts talking about being on one side of a fence or the other, whereas we know full well that there need and should be no fence whatsoever. Having spent twenty years at a Bishop's House in a seat of administration, I am inevitably conscious of the supremely important work which has to be carried out by selfless men at headquarters endeavouring to give service to those in the field, where they would probably rather be themselves. They are not helped by sneering references to a "curia". On the other hand, having been for an all too short time a parish priest, and for an even shorter time a curate, I am also aware of the sense of exasperation felt by those in the field at the apparent lack of understanding by those at the "sending out" end of the difficulties in which the pastoral life of a parish has to be carried through. I do not believe that any one person or even any one of the "us and them" mentality can put it right. There has to be a genuine desire on the part of all parties to take every reasonable step to bridge that gap.

It is when one goes into details that one can easily

sound smug and over confident and it is not improbable that, in some of the experiments which must be made in bridging the gap, one or other of us will burn his fingers. But the experiments must be made and whilst they are being made there must be patience, trust and a real attempt at understanding by all parties concerned. If we were starting completely from scratch, it would be so much easier. But attitudes of mind have hardened, even where the heart has not, and such attitudes of mind can attach too much or too little importance to gestures which are meant to do no more than signify the general intentions of those who make them.

At the lowest level, take the case of the colour of a bishop's cassock buttons: who can pretend that this seriously makes any difference to the future of the Church or to the way in which we conduct ourselves? Yet if purple is to some priests and people as a red rag to a bull, I will gladly cast it on one side. If traditional forms of salutation are a difficulty for some people, then I welcome their abandonment. But let us remember that these things only have a significance when we understand that the desire is to remove obstacles to the proper relationship between us. What undoubtedly is important is that the bishop should remain so closely in touch with his priests that their changing views and the changing circumstances in which they have to work can always be known to him. Equally the priests must be understanding of the difficulty for a bishop to remain completely in touch if the priests themselves will not be frank with him. There has to be this mutual confidence and freedom of expression and good communication. There has to be a fraternal love which should lie at the very heart of the brotherhood of the priesthood.

What structure can be created to foster this relationship? In Council terms there is the recommendation for the establishment of a council of priests and in most dioceses this has already been carried out. Its purpose is to assist the bishop in his rule of the diocese, and not to serve as some form of clerical trade union. We have already seen three of the main tasks facing a bishop: to preach the word of God, to foster right relationships between himself, the priests and the laity, and to coordinate pastoral activity. In all these the council of priests must help. But they will only do so effectively if we realise that their authority and strength comes not merely from the powers given to them by the bishop but also from the degree of confidence which they enjoy amongst those whom they are to serve. For this reason the elective principle must be incorporated.

What about the relationship between priests and laity? The layman has responsibility from his very baptism. Therefore let us be clear from the beginning that it is not a quesion of letting a layman "help". We hear well intentioned men speaking of the need of trying to *involve* the laity in the life of the parish, as if they were some form of immigrant to be admitted to an ecclesiastical community. Pius XII used to say of the laity: "You are the Church". We have to work so that the parish priest will open his arms to those entrusted to his pastoral care and say to them: "Brothers and sisters in Christ, we are the Church. I have a specific task to fulfil in our community. So have you. But we must work together to carry out the mission of the Church here in this parish".

Is this too idealistic? It may be over-optimistic for two reasons: first, because we need not imagine that all the laity are falling over their feet to play their full part in the mission of the Church, and secondly, because the clergy have been brought up on such inspired phrases as "Let the laity be the auxiliaries of the hierarchy" — a consecrated phrase, papal in origin though without claim of infallibility. As usual there are two extreme forms of trouble. There are those who imagine that the layman's task in the Church is to be enclosed within the small expanse stretching from taking the collections to calling out the numbers at bingo. On the other hand there are many who have not realised the apostolic possibilities of much of the work in which the layman is engaged. Perhaps because there is at present a reaction against joining organisations, there is a growing realisation that it can be a good and Christian thing for individuals and even groups of individuals to meet certain essential needs of the community. One is encouraged by the number of schools in which one finds pupils being brought to an understanding of the crying needs of old people. Somehow we have to ensure that priest and people alike realise that the layman has a part to play in every aspect of the Church's life: in spiritual matters as well as in secular matters: in taking an active part in the liturgy as well as being concerned in the branch activity of a trade union.

My own strong belief is that once priests realise the width of the layman's apostolate as well as the expertise he may place at the service of the Church, there will be less fear lest the lay apostolate means letting the laity get control of the money. Similarly once laymen understand fully the extent of their apostolate and come to appreciate the use to which they may place their talents, enthusiasm and zeal, there will be less of the frustration which often so damages the good relationships between priests and people that parochial life can become restricted to sacramental administration. What is the answer? We all of us need formation in the ideas about the way in which the layman can play his part in the life of the Church at parish level. That formation must be achieved by priests and people working it out together. This does mean a fairly radical change in many places. It also means that priest and people have to take a radical look at the problems facing their parish together and together see what is the best way of tackling them.

I have dealt at length with possible structures but let us remember that these things are means to an end. Before the Church can truly fulfil her mission to the world, there must be this real renewal in the relationship between the members of the people of God: bishop, priests, religious and laity. We must work together, we must pray together, we must worship together and certainly we must talk together. We must even be prepared to put up with the jibes of those who say: "I was hungry and you formed a discussion group". We must learn to think and to plan for the future as well as to administer passing first aid.

Relationships as well as structures are means to an end. I will close by quoting from Karl Rahner who, in his book *Mission and Grace*, seems to have appreciated this point: "Hold fast to each other in brotherly love: live with each other in mutual respect and helpfulness; honour each other's gifts and talents, even when they are not your own kind. For the one Spirit imparts to each a different gift, and the whole Body of Christ is never present in one single member. And even fighting for the right against the wrong does not justify the use of poisoned weapons or an attitude that contradicts the spirit of the Gospel. Strike out boldly along new paths in pastoral work. But if these paths do not lead to the altar of God, to the confessional and to the prie-dieu, they are not the paths of Christ leading to life".

EUCHARIST AND COMMUNITY

I was once given the sad task of going to visit a seminarist in a large mental hospital. For a time he thought he was St Paul and was determined that in his personal ship-wreck it would not be a case of "women and children first". When I went to see him he had another problem. To help their patients in the matter of human relationships the hospital authorities arranged a dance every Saturday night in which all patients were obliged to participate. The seminarist told me that he objected to this. "There I am", he said, "out on the floor, trying to talk sweet nothings to someone with whom the only thing I have in common is that we are both of the opposite sex".

I sometimes feel that the one thing all parish priests have in common is that each one is convinced that his own parish is — for better or for worse — absolutely unique. There may be other things in common, such as the grace of orders, but this business of "my parish is different" and "that couldn't work here", this is the outward sign of the true parish priest. But all parish priests should be able to agree that a parish is a coming together of people with a common purpose and a unifying trait. A parish is intended to be a means by which this community, this coming together, is achieved. I say *a* means rather than *the* means because obviously there can be communities

23

larger or smaller than a parish: it also raises the very interesting question about how large a parish can be without losing its community character or purpose.

There are no absolute rules about it: geography and density of population have to be taken into consideration. But when a thing is so large that its members have little in common, when the people are so many, so diverse or so scattered, that they cannot know one another; when they can feel so remote from the heart of the community that they have no sense of responsibility towards it, no capacity to share in it, no sense of belonging; then the so-called community and its nominal members have become unhealthy as well as unwieldy. It is this sort of thing which leads economists, industrialists and politicians to say "Small is beautiful".

"Now be fair", the parish priest may say quite reasonably. "If I have a church to seat 1500 people, I cannot pull it down. In any case I need a church that size to get all my people in. And I need that number of people to give a collection large enough to cope with the inflationary costs of the plant . . ." There is not much point in my repeating well-known problems. Numbers and circumstances may differ. But at the end of it, it is still people, a worshipping pilgrim people, with Jesus Christ working in and through their human relationships. The parish, or whatever structure may be devised, is a means to that end. No matter what size this parish-community may be, Christ is the common bond and his mission is the unifying trait.

There are dozen of ways in which a parish, large or small, can be animated to deserve that "living parish" label. But the real difference priests are having to face today has little to do directly with the problems of size. The real difference is the new emphasis or insight into the nature of the Church. Basically what has happened is that there has been a shift in emphasis from a body, in which there was largely passive membership, to a living organism, in which we are required actively to respond to Christ's call to share in his saving work.

Let me enlarge on this point briefly for it is at the heart of our understanding of the Church community, of which the parish community is a microcosm. It is vital to our understanding of how Christ enters into the new relationships which have had to be established between bishop, priests and people. It is basic to our whole concept of the parish as a eucharistic community. It is no good pretending that the Council has not happened or that it was quite unnecessary. I remember very well being told by a parish priest outside Cork that he knew all his parishioners and that only two did not go to Mass — that was the same, he said, before the Vatican Council as after it: so what need had he of the Second Vatican Council and liturgical renewal? But the fact remains that in the last years the world has changed. There are different outlooks and influences. The Second Vatican Council did take place and there are now different emphases on our membership of the Church. It is no good our wishing it had not happened or burying our heads and believing that the winds of change will blow out.

What exactly has happened to make things different from 1960 when the first of the pre-Conciliar preparatory commissions began to meet? What has happened to the Church — and therefore to the parish which is a microcosm of the Church? There can be little doubt that prior to the Second Vatican Council the Church was seen by the laity as a body of which they had membership and in which certain things were done to them or for them. The liturgy was a good example. The priest came out to the altar, turned his back on them and got on with the job, admittedly on their behalf, even if they could not see, hear or understand what he was saying or doing. It was enough that he did it and that they were there. They might be able to keep up with him in their missals if they had them or they could pray away at the same time, struggling to get the knot out of their rosaries. But the main thing was that the priest got on with it. The laity were largely passive attenders. If they could not get into the Church, they

25

C

could prop up the wall outside, though not, as the moralists told us, at a distance of more than forty paces away from the other worshippers. In the sacramental system the emphasis was on *ex opere operato* — confirm the child as soon as possible after first communion and make no demand of any response beyond his having apparently reached the age of reason: wait till the sick are in proximate danger of death before anointing, consciousness is of no consequence. It was all done to you. Inevitably this led to a largely clerical Church, with the laity in support and with almost all representatives of the Church wearing a dog-collar. The way was at least open for functionaries and formalism.

As a result of the theology of *Lumen Gentium*, we now see the Church as a living organism, a live body to which you actively belong and where you are, as a member of Christ's body, expected to respond — both as an individual and as a member of the community — to Christ's call to share in his work which he entrusted to his Church. The emphasis has moved away from what is done to you to that response, to the *ex opere operantis* aspect. Again this is most clearly evident in our participative liturgy, in the sacraments where the capacity to respond to the grace held out is seen to be of great importance. If you like, the shift has been from passive to active, from the almost exclusively clerical to the broadly ecclesial.

That is the real difference: it is a consequence of the developed theology of the Church and I believe it to be more important to understand why the liturgy has had to be revised or renewed than to place emphasis on the "how do you do it" aspect. But it may help if I treat of some aspects of the celebration of the eucharist in which the laity are now being asked to participate and respond, rather than just "be there", which was the adequate slogan of the past.

I often think that it was no accident that Pope John decided that the Sacred Liturgy should be the first subject studied by the Fathers of the Second Vatican Council.

Once they had understood how God's people came together in worship they were in good shape to study the nature and mission of the Church. Indeed if you study the Constitution on Sacred Liturgy you will find the basics of the great Constitution on the Church. The vital quotation is from article 21 from the Constitution *Sacrosanctum Concilium*:

"In order that the Christian people may more certainly derive an abundance of graces from the Sacred Liturgy, holy mother Church desires to undertake with great care a general restoration of the liturgy itself. For the liturgy is made up of unchangeable elements divinely instituted, and of elements subject to change ... In restoration both texts and rites should be drawn up to express more clearly the holy things which they signify. The Christian people, as far as is possible, should be able to understand them with ease and take part in them fully, actively, and as a community".

It will be useful to follow this with the relevant implementing text from the General Instruction of the Roman Missal in 1970:

"It is therefore of the greatest importance that the celebration of the Mass, the Lord's Supper, be so arranged that everybody — ministers and people — may take their own proper part in it ... the best way to achieve this will be to consider the particular circumstances and character of the community and then to organise the details of the celebration in a way that will lead them to full, active and conscious participation. This implies a participation that will involve them in both body and soul, and will inspire them in faith, hope and charity. This is what the Church desires; this is what the nature of the celebration demands: it is this to which the faithful have both the right and duty by reason of their baptism" (Nos. 2 and 3).

So the people have to understand; they have to take part fully as members of a community: and the celebration

27

must be organised to fit the character and circumstances of the community. Note the shift: not just build a church large enough so that they can attend whilst Mass is offered in the sanctuary; but ensure that the liturgy is celebrated in a way that will enable all those who are present to respond. Note also "celebrate". Not *say* Mass or even *sing* Mass, but *celebrate* the Mass, a celebration of the Lord's Supper.

Am I just playing with words? What are the consequences of this new emphasis? This is where the parish priest may wish to start saying: "You couldn't do that in my parish: the church isn't right for it and the people wouldn't want it".

First, let us take this idea of the celebration itself. If you were planning a celebration you would ask "Where shall we have it?" It would have to match the numbers so you have not much choice. But then you would make the place ready — for the celebration and the kind of celebration it was going to be. This is why we must work to the principle that the place must be made to fit the celebration, not dictate the shape of the celebration. This in turn is why the churches and sanctuaries, unless quite new, must usually be re-ordered for the revised rite of the Mass. This is not iconoclasm. It is getting our priorities right. The liturgy can sometimes become an almost ridiculous if not near-sacrilegious obstacle race if one attempts a full celebration of the new rite amidst the old setting.

Again with a celebration, and a community celebration at that, the host or organiser welcomes those who come to take part and sees them away or says goodbye at the end. There may be lots of doors to a church but there is usually a main entrance. It is difficult for the celebrant to be there at the door when people arrive, though if there is more than one priest in the parish one of them can often do it. Celebrant or no, the priest can and ought to make for the main door as the people leave: he need not worry about going straight to the door in his vestments, if necessary. If the people sing a final hymn, and then the priest goes to the door with a procession the people will usually wait for him. Once they realise that this is the normal thing, they will always give him time to reach the porch. There he will collect more practical information, he will learn and impart more pastoral truths in the few minutes it takes for the church to empty than at almost any other time. Most important the people will see that the priest, who offers the Mass in their name and leads their celebration, is interested in them as people.

A final point about celebration: it must be well-prepared. The best way for a priest to prepare for Mass nowadays is to prepare the Mass: to read those readings the night before so that he may understand the under-lying theme of the liturgy of the word and thereby be able to lead his people. We can all lose the place but it is sad if someone cannot find the place or reads the wrong day or the wrong year because he has not looked at it before-hand. Only in this way can a priest really have the con-fidence and understanding to lead the people in the community celebration. No longer is it enough for him to come out, open the book, find the place and then just read it or say it. The Mass is to be prayed and the people led in prayer. To do this we priests must know what we are doing and where we are going. Let the homily be a drawing out of the meaning of God's word in the Holy Scripture assigned to the day, not just another sermon from the syllabus or the book of sermons, regardless of the day. If the priest has to get it all in inside thirty minutes, to contain the people with a succession of Masses, this is the time to build a new church.

If everyone is to take part in the celebration — as members of the community — that means that the laity also must have the opportunity to play their part. If it is claimed that they do not want to, or they cannot read well enough, or it would be invidious to single people out, then we are confessing that they have not understood the role which the Church says is theirs: in accordance with their vocation or ministry. Remember those words from the general instruction: "a full, active, conscious participation, which the Church desires and to which the faithful have the right and duty according to their baptism".

Clearly all this may seem a pipe-dream unless we can achieve that phrase in the Constitution on the Sacred Liturgy: "The Christian people, as far as possible, should be able to understand them with ease and take part in them fully, actively and as a community". Under God, the priest will succeed in so far as the people understand. They will understand in so far as there is explanation of the "whys" as well as the "what has to be done". This should be offered with enthusiasm rather than apologies for what have come to be known as "the changes". It is not just a case of "You tell us what to do, Father, and we will do it". There has to be responsible participation and therefore more is required. I am not saying that in the past the people did not know what it was all about. But there is a big difference between knowing in general terms what the priest was doing "up there" whilst perhaps you prayed, and taking a full, active and conscious part in what, each with his own ministry, we are doing together — celebrating Christ's death and resurrection. It is a celebration which is at the heart of the parish-community.

AUTHORITY IN THE CHURCH

In the years following the Council and, in particular, following the publication of *Humanae Vitae*, a key issue in the Church has been authority. Ironically, in the years before the Council many converts joined the Church because of her authority; in the present day a number of people leave the Church out of opposition to the same authority. In both instances it is likely that there has been an inadequate appreciation of the nature of authority in the Church and the manner in which it is or should be exercised. Perhaps the greatest difficulty arises in the inevitable confusion in our minds between authority as exercised in secular government and Christian authority in its ecclesial context. Even with those who exercise it, there is sometimes a confusion between the two. History tells us of kings who claimed divine right and of popes who exercised temporal dominion in their own states. Our difficulties with authority today are not quite the same. They are certainly more subtle.

It seems important to make a clear distinction between the sources of authority and the manner of its exercise. Rosemary Haughton, in an essay in her *Dialogue with Cardinal Heenan*, wrote, "Authority is not the same thing as power. The usual reaction to this statement is 'No, of course it isn't, authority in the Church means service'. But this comment shows just as deep a misunderstanding of

31

authority as the assumption that authority is another word for power. Authority in the Church has the same function as authority anywhere else, and neither power nor service expresses its nature. They simply describe ways of exercising it."

This distinction was also made by Pope Paul when talking on 27th January, 1968, to the Roman Rota: "Owing to the fact that the concept of authority in the Church is often reduced to its *raison d'etre*, which is that of service, care must be taken lest the origin of that authority be misunderstood, as if it came from the community of the faithful and did not derive its superior source from divine law: in other words care must be taken lest this efficient principle be confused with the purpose for which Christ established it, that is, for the guidance and salvation of the People of God."

God has chosen to give guidance to his people supremely through the life and teaching of his Son, Jesus Christ. That teaching of Christ is their way of life, not just a manner of Church worship. They have been told to take it to all nations. In this immense task they are given confidence by the promise of Christ's abiding presence in the Church which he instituted.

God has entrusted to his Church the mediation to all ages of the word and work of Christ. Lest his promise should fail through human weakness, Christ's own presence and the work of his Spirit in the Church ensure that his teaching, though understood more fully as century succeeds century, remains intact and uncorrupted, whatever be the shortcomings of individuals. Christ himself was the fulness of God's revelation to man and there is no new revelation to be made. All God's saving messages are contained in the teaching his Church hands out, teaching which finds its basic expression in the gospels. With Scripture goes the Church's living memory of her Lord. It is the handing on, to which succeeding generations contribute, that we call tradition.

It is from Scripture and this tradition that the Church

continues to draw her teaching of the good news of Jesus Christ. In this teaching God so assists her that the whole Church can never fail in its belief, whatever may be the shortcomings of individuals. The Church's teaching office, the handing on of the Gospel, is entrusted to the college of bishops, as successors of Christ's chosen apostles. When this college, in full union with its head, the Pope, gives definitive, doctrinal or moral teaching, God's assistance assures its freedom from error. Because the Pope, as successor of St Peter, is head of that college, his own official (or *ex cathedra*) decisions on matter of Christian faith and moral practice — decisions that have, of course, to be made with all due human care and consideration — such decisions are themselves guaranteed this preservation from error. This we call infallibility.

We believe that this is the way chosen by God whereby the purity of this good news may be ensured amidst the changing world of thought and opinion. It is in this setting of Christ's abiding presence in the Church that I place the whole question of authority in that Church.

The divine source of authority is not to be identified with the manner of its exercise. But it should be linked with it. To understand this it is helpful to consider also the idea of authenticity. The word "authority", as Rosemary Haughton has pointed out so thoughtfully, has the same root as "author". When we speak of an authority, we mean someone who can truthfully represent the mind and character of the author. It is not a matter of power or even necessarily of cleverness, but simply of being close to the source. Christ spoke with authority about human life because of his close relationship with the author of human life, and his very way of speaking showed the assurance and conviction which came from this closeness.

So in this sense authority is about a relationship to the author. You may have a scientific authority or a political authority: he is a means whereby other members of the community are able to achieve a greater knowledge of and relationship to the source. A genuine political authority will be able to make an authentic interpretation of his party's aims and policy. This idea of relationship with the source is immensely important in trying to understand Christian authority.

Rosemary Haughton also writes: "Authority is the community's reference to source. It is its self-explanation, both the sign of its nature and the means whereby it accomplishes its purposes as a community. It is true of any community. It is true of the Church. Authority in the Church is the means whereby the community realises its relationship to Christ its author. It is the way in which it explains to itself what it is, what it is for, and what it must do about it".

I find this approach most satisfying in showing us how authority should be exercised. We speak of Christ the servant. Those exercising authority in the Church, be they Pope, Reverend Mother, or the head of a family, must give the authentic service of their ministry to other members of the community. It also helps us to determine in our own and other ages of the Church's history what sometimes goes wrong in the exercise of authority: how we allow self in various forms to obscure our role as an authentic means of relationship with Christ. This connection between author, authority and authenticity can also help to fill the missing link between the hierarchical structure of the Church and the co-responsibility of the baptised, the people of God.

The Conciliar emphasis on the true nature of the Church, its one mission, its different ministries, between which there is equality of dignity — with all members sharing in the task given by Christ to his Church — this has inevitably affected relationships between the members and indeed the ministries. This is not a denial or change of authority in the Church. It is rather the occasion when the manner of the Church's exercise of authority must be re-examined and to some extent re-thought. The authority, as such, given to the Church is indestructible and incorruptible. But the concrete forms in which this authority appears do not necessarily share this incorruptibility. These forms are capable of reform and development but the test of whether a manner of authority is genuine is ultimately the New Testament, in which the original grant of authority to the Church is seen.

It is argued sometimes that the manner of exercise of authority in the Church is medieval: at least that it has been on the defensive since the Reformation. Historically this is not surprising but the changes in structures of dialogue made in the Second Vatican Council are a clear recognition of the fact that the Church is incarnate in the world, and that in her structures she is influenced by general trends of thought and behaviour in society as a whole. At this time these trends are best described by association with the vogue word "participation". It finds expression in many forms. Martin Luther King once said that when the individual no longer feels that he is participating in the improvement of society, he no longer feels a sense of responsibility to it.

In the Church, with its hierarchical structures, the cor-responsibility of all the faithful is the means whereby the authentic witness of Christ, preserved and even more deeply understood by authority, can be given expression to the whole world. It is the means whereby, with the development of right relationships, individuals contribute to the whole, supplying and filling in for the inevitable human weak-nesses and inadequacies of individuals to whom, in one measure or another, authority in the Church is entrusted. The Church is not the same as democracy. But a true understanding of authority in the Church necessitates the incorporation of the notion of the corresponsibility of the faithful in the true mission of the Church, towards which authority is directed. This is why consultation and structures of dialogue are important for our understanding of authority in a co-responsible Church.

Secular tension as well as methods of government are often reflected in the Church. Sometimes the tensions in contemporary society, when understood, can help to throw light on those experienced in the Church. Take the example of a bishop today. In many ways there are similarities between the way he has to exercise authority and the authority of a contemporary father of a family. "In exercising his office as father and pastor" we are told in the Council's Decree on the Pastoral Care of Dioceses, "the bishop should be with his people as one who serves, as a good shepherd who knows his sheep and whose sheep know him, as a true father who excels in his love and solicitude for all, to whose divinely conferred authority all readily submit. He should so unite and mould his flock into one family that all, conscious of their duties, may live and act in the communion of charity" (*Christus Dominus*, 16).

In many ways a bishop, in his exercise of authority, must be a father of faith, not merely giving witness to his own faith, but by word and example building up the faith of his people. To speak of the episcopate as a "fatherhood of faith" is not to advocate paternalism. The unchanging apostolic office of a bishop has to be lived in accordance with the needs of the place and the times: and these are times in which there are many changes in the role of a contemporary father towards his family.

Today the father (and the bishop) must listen and be seen to listen before he can instruct. He must be patient, understanding but clearly leading others to right decisions by precepts but most of all by example. His role is supportive, even though he himself needs support. He must be sensitive to the pressures under which the other members of his family are labouring. With vision and discernment, and a nice balance of human and humble understanding, he must try to help them to get their priorities right. Though some of his children may choose to leave home — more because it is the "done" thing than for any valid reason — he must patiently strive to maintain contact and keep alive Christ's presence amongst even the most prodigal of them. In this he must be a sign of compassion, justice, truth and hope.

One last point with regard to this vital question of authority in the Church. No one can deny the periodic breakdown of the exercise of authority due to human weakness. When this happens the issue of conscience cannot be ignored. Here too we should turn to the example of Christ, in his conflict with the authorities of the chosen people. Whilst on occasion he in conscience set the law to one side, he never denied the validity of that authority. Admittedly Jesus knew himself to be the Lord of the law but he knew also the voice of the Father speaking directly to him. In face of real conscientious difficulty about response to the non-infallible use of authority, we must follow Christ. Before all else, in our efforts to unite our conscience to the dictate of authority, we must open our hearts to the Father, that we may know and do his will in all things. And even if, quite exceptionally, we may have on occasion to decide to refuse to carry out an instruction which we feel we cannot do without offence to conscience, yet we continue to acknowledge the authority of Christ in the Church.

Karl Rahner, once again, has the word for it: "Even if a command is given in the right spirit, and obedience is given with a prayerful spirit, conflicts are possible and no prioristic rule will put them out of bounds, since we are all finite men liable to error, and indissolubly bound to our conscience. Yet he who is led by the Spirit of Christ and seeks not his own, remains committed obediently to God in faith in this conflict and is in the peace of Christ" (*Christ as the exemplar of obedience*).

EXPENDABILITY AND PRIESTHOOD

It is easy to be wise after the event. Hindsight is almost inevitably selective. From eleven years of training in junior and senior seminary I remember both good and bad: surprise at those who gave up on the way, surprise at some who continued, the slow realisation that "I have chosen you, you have not chosen me".

Of events immediately prior to my ordination just before D-day in 1944, I remember best the cumulative final advice given me by three members of the seminary staff. I had been quite seriously ill. Cambridge and the long-threatened role of priest-schoolmaster must be abandoned. The doctor had advised a country curacy in a parish needing one and a half priests.

Fearing boredom from inactivity I approached my confessor. "No need to worry," he said. "No educated man need ever be bored. You can always read". I looked a little doubtfully at his shelves of Boyer, S.J., and Wodehouse, P.G. "No need to worry", confirmed his more cynical colleague, "The only thing you can be sure of as a priest is that in twelve months' time you will not be doing what now you imagine you will be doing". My third consultant was the spiritual director. He was a holy old man whose many years in the Catholic Missionary Society had not cured his broken-English accent. He contented himself

39

with pastoral advice. "Make your parish priest your daddy", he said.

Mercifully in the diocese of my adoption there was no vacant country curacy. So with supreme abandon I was posted to London W.8. Eleven months later medical opinion was evidently lost in the diocesan archives and most reluctantly I found myself the Archbishop's Private Secretary. When questioned I had confessed myself an inexperienced driver, an indifferent typist and an inadequate linguist. "Good", said the Archbishop, "you have one qualification I am looking for. You obviously don't want the job". My appointment would be provisional for a year.

Nineteen years and three Archbishops later I emerged to become a parish priest. I had a particular assignment in the East End of London and with my first team of priests we worked out a five-year-plan. After eighteen months I was appointed bishop of the diocese from which I had been excardinated for tonsure exactly twenty-five years earlier.

Possibly you may feel that the cynic has proved his point. I would be sad if this potted biography suggested that I now shared his cynicism. To me perhaps the most important lesson I have learned in my experience of priesthood is that in the cause of Christ and of him crucified the priest must try to accept that he is expendable.

This may seem soul-less and impersonal, making demands beyond the call of duty. To some it may seem a thinly-disguised pleading of the case for discipline and obedience. Business efficiency experts will argue the relative merits of a mobile labour force as against job-satisfaction. This is not my point. To share in the priesthood of Christ leaves no room for compromise. It demands total dedication, the total gift of self.

To be expendable must mean willingness to be used, joyfully and completely, in the furtherance of Christ's saving mission. The measure in which a priest holds back from this is the extent to which he fails to be a channel of grace. In his attempts to hold heaven and earth together, he will at times be stretched to near breaking-point. So were the arms of Christ on the cross. A priest's apparent failure in the eyes of others can in itself render him more Christ-like. Somehow and at some time in his ministry the priest must come to terms with this.

The acceptance of this idea of expendability does not imply wastefulness, the abuse or neglect of talents. The suppression of self does not absolve us from the need to develop and use our personality, to equip ourselves with the knowledge we need to serve the particular interests of our people. This obligation lies with the priest himself as much as it does with those responsible for his assignment.

The very expendability of a priest places immense responsibility on those by whose authority he ministers. There are willing horses among the clergy, as in every walk of life. There are also some who for reasons of personal security desire to dig in at all costs. The hard realisation that the best man is seldom available for the right post just when he is wanted renders the willing horse vulnerable to second-best posting.

Sometimes this is inevitable. The people are often the sufferers. In considering the needs of both priest and parishioners there has to be a proper balance. Where resources are limited there will on occasion be square pegs in round holes: or almost square pegs in nearly round holes. The surgeon's knife is seldom the best treatment. The bishop can do much to ease the pain and sometimes to achieve by adjustment a better fit of the same peg in the same hole.

Between brethren there must undoubtedly be a certain equity in the bearing of heavy burdens. A knowledgeable choice of broad backs is not enough. Common sense and very human considerations usually demand that a priest be asked his willingness to accept this or that appointment. He should certainly be given the chance to explain if there are unknown or personal reasons against it. Sometimes there may be almost no option on either side, but the priest should at least have the reason for the proposed appointment explained to him personally.

41

If appointments are made on a personal basis, preferably by the bishop, many affronts and causes for discontent can be overcome. That said, my experience is that in the end most priests desire to be at the disposition of the bishop whose responsibility it is to provide for the people. No priest relishes a system whereby he is offered the fifth preference for a difficult assignment already widely but unsuccessfully hawked around amongst his colleagues.

Of the five appointments I have held as a priest, only one would I gladly have chosen. We are seldom the best judges of our own capabilities. For a priest the phrase "No man is an island" means that he is only one small part of the body of Christ the priest. Mindful of St Paul's analogy, he knows that those who share in the priesthood of Christ are interdependent. No one limb can do it all. Nor, if Christ is the head, can the individual simply choose the particular task or form of ministry which he happens to prefer.

There are many different ways in which the priestly ministry is to be exercised today. The need for a certain experimentation will not be best met by the individual's choosing to go it alone or doing his own things regardless of other priests or the needs of the local Church. Good organisation and efficient coordination are not the only issues at stake when it comes to the development of clergy. For all the development we are witnessing today in the methods of appointing priests, nothing can displace the priest's willingness to be expendable as the needs of others may dictate.

When I left my last parish I was driven away by a priest past the junior school. All the children and their teachers were out in the street to wave good-bye. A number of supporting "mums" had gathered by the gates to speed me on my way. I felt emotionally drained. My colleague, who must have seen my feelings, offered me no sympathy. "Never forget", he said, "that all this lies behind a line and a half in the Clerical Appointments column in the *Universe*".

Years in the priesthood serve to emphasise the immense

importance of human relationships as well as spiritual relationships. Celibacy must be seen as a gift to God rather than an administrative advantage. In spite of all the snide remarks about crabbed bachelors — and we should not overlook the dangers of a bachelor's temptations to selfishness and eccentricity — my experience has been that the Lord rewards a celibate life not merely with a unique spiritual relationship with himself but also with the opportunity for enhanced human relationships with other priests and with the laity.

I suspect that my first parish priest would have been even more embarrassed than I by the suggestion that I should regard his as my "Daddy". He was shy to the point that his defence mechanism was interpreted by those who did not know him as aggressiveness. We became firm friends from the moment when, a few days after my arrival, I flung him on the floor as he hung out of a window to try to see a flying bomb which seconds later scored a near miss on the presbytery. I fell on top of him just before the glass covered both of us. The barrier of shyness was not the only thing broken that day.

He taught his curates that the basis of our relationship must be trust, rooted in understanding of our different characters and capabilities. If you acquired a job you were expected to tell him and the others. If you were assigned one, you were left to get on with it as your own responsibility. Recognising that you were more likely to seek advice from the senior curate than from himself, he never enquired how you were progressing. Just as you imagined he had forgotten or might not care, he would drop a remark indicating that he knew very well how much or how little you had done.

When I was threatened with a move, he wrote to the Vicar General to protest. When some weeks later I was "told" by the Archbishop, he was the first to help me to accept the situation. It was the harder when some years later I was sent by authority to persuade him to retire owing to ill-health. He protested that I had been sent, thanked me for having told him and added that I was quite right. My original assignment to him was another example of the importance of a first appointment.

Excellent as were the relationships within that presbytery, I remember thinking how strange it was that I scarcely knew the priests in the neighbouring parishes, many of them religious. Deanery meetings were no more than an irrelevant formality, rapidly dispensed with. I learned that the number of priests living in an area had little to do with isolation. A priest had a certain number of priest-friends but the idea of inter-parochial responsibility, let alone priestly brotherhood, was almost non-existent. You got on with your own job and that was enough. Contact with other priests, save your fellow curates, was for days off.

In many ways this attitude was the cause of clericalism. Working with other priests, especially if that happy state of affairs covers a wide area, turns a merely professional relationship into an active expression of brotherhood. The relationship between priests may be by virtue of order. It finds meaning and is elevated above a caste-system once it takes the form of collaboration in ministry. The fact that it is a ministry of service to the laity is the greatest safeguard against clericalism.

I may have been unusually fortunate in the priests with whom I have had the opportunity to work. They have not always been kindred spirits but I have nearly always first found brotherhood with them in pastoral ministry. Thereafter it has been possible to see the consequences of that relationship. The sharing which is of the essence in all team work has to be of the comprehensive variety; if there is no interest or activity in the parish which is exclusively your responsibility, you soon discover that, as in the best of families, there are few things which cannot and will not be shared. If this can include spirituality, rather than just pastoral techniques, all concerned will be the richer.

This should not be interpreted as monasticism or clericalism, any more than pastoral ministry should be equated with parish life. I was ordained for the service of the people. My life as a priest — and indeed my relationship with other priests — has been enriched by deep friendship with lay men and women with whom I have had contact through priestly service and collaboration in the life of the Church. For all the fact that they have opened their doors to me, I have realised that for their sake too the presbytery must be my home.

It used to be said that you could tell the date of a man's ordination by the books on his shelves. I suspect that there may have been some truth in this some twenty or so years ago. There was a sameness about the appearance of seminary text-books, especially if their pages remained uncut. The tweedy-covered issues from the Catholic Book-a-Month Club often accounted for not inconsiderable footage of presbytery reading-matter in the '30s and '40s. "*I remember Maynooth*" did not always proclaim the truth about its owner but later on guide-books and maps indicated the advent of continental holidays for the clergy.

The last ten years have witnessed the transfer of many of these dust-laden classics from the parish priest's study to the presbytery waiting room. A survey of a priest's bookshelves today, though no longer indicative of ordination dates, will nevertheless tell you a great deal. It will not always reveal his precise position when the theological compass is boxed. Allowance must sometimes be made for window-dressing and even for good intentions defeated by late night television or an easy surrender to sleep. But as a rule it will tell you most of what you need to know about his attitudes.

In these post-Conciliar years a willingness to study new approaches to dogmatic, moral and pastoral theology has been a fair indication of a priest's openness to the Spirit in the Church at this time. A response to the Vatican Council's call for renewal has inevitably involved study. The presbytery bookshelf is usually some indication of this.

If, in spite of my confessor's forecast, I have seldom been driven by boredom to Wodehouse or Boyer, I have found it absolutely essential to read as regularly as possible "both friend and foe in all our strife". In the seminary we were taught "subjects", usually presented distinct from each other rather as we were apt to see the various vocations and ministries in the Church in their separate compartments. The new emphasis on the unity of the Church in her membership and mission has led to an integration of the different fields of the theological learning. The resultant advent of the so-called paperback theology has, I suspect, been for most priests a welcome substitute for the distant custodianship of the text-books and lecture notes of old.

The new stress on biblical understanding has meant a satisfying change from exegetical theorising and an opportunity to relate scripture to worship. In many ways the abandonment of the "weights and measures" approach to moral theology has brought realism to our efforts to shed the light of the Gospel on the world as we know it. The social revolution in society today has shown the poverty of our sociological preparation in the past. We might as well admit that liturgical renewal has served to remind us that twenty years ago over-much interest in pastoral liturgy exposed a man to accusations of eccentricity. To be enthused about the lay apostolate made it likely that one would be labelled as an anti-clerical crank.

There has been much to read about and to re-think. I may thank God that for me there was the opportunity for renewal of heart and mind in the Council itself. I have only to glance at my diaries of that period to realise the influences to which I was exposed each day. But to try to keep abreast with what was happening then, it was essential to read, often very late at night. To make sure that the process of renewal and development did not stop in 1965 it has proved vital to continue that reading.

Few priests find it easy to set aside the time needed to read all they require to know. So much is published, it is difficult to know what books and reviews to choose. Insofar as a priest is willing to try to read and weigh carefully the renewal that is taking place in theological writing — and to preserve a sensible balance in his choice of books — so he will achieve an openness to the Spirit which is not the same thing as a spiritual vacuum. Such an attitude amongst priests will be of great importance to the Church in the future. It will do much to build up the right relationship amongst her members.

So perhaps after all I was fortunate in the three pieces of advice given me before ordination. Things may not have worked out quite as my consultors anticipated. They certainly fitted no pattern I could have conceived. Even then I know that no priest can write of the supreme experience which is granted to him by the Lord: things of the spirit and which are for him alone. Trembling with presumption, he can only repeat the words of St John: "There were many other things that Jesus did; if all were written down, the world itself, I suppose, would not hold all the books that would have to be written" (Jn 21:25).

COMPASSION IN PRIESTLY COMMITMENT

When in the past I have referred to the expendability of priests I have sometimes been accused of being callous. Perhaps it has suggested that priests are appointed and used without adequate thought for their health or capacity or even their likes and dislikes: that they can be *used up* quite impersonally, as if they were inanimate plugs to stem the tide of paganism that otherwise would wash over whole territories before it breaks upon the rock of Peter.

What I have meant is in fact that there is nothing of self that the priest can retain if he is to serve God in the priestly ministry and give himself also to the service of God's people. This total offering of self is necessary if he is to be for others an open channel of communication in their approach to Christ. Almost certainly this total offering is also necessary for his happiness as a priest. What he holds back is an obstacle to those he must serve and a block in his relationship with Christ whose priesthood he shares.

If a young man comes to see me to discuss whether he should offer himself for the priesthood, I leave him in no doubt about the nature of his gift of self. "There can be no strings attached" I tell him. "The Lord wants the lot from you. It may mean blood, sweat and tears from you, but you will grow close to Christ in his agony; and if there are tears, they will be tears of joy".

God is never outdone in generosity. But there can be no compromise. A priest must be willing to go where he is most needed and do what is most needed. It is true that the bishop must make the best use of his priest's talents and that happiness contributes to the effectiveness of ministry. But it will always be the better service of the people which will determine where he goes and what he does.

Some years ago a parish priest came to see me. He had built a school and a church and was in his late forties. He could reasonably have expected to be allowed to stay where he was to enjoy the fruits of his labours and the gratitude of his people. But he saw the danger in this and feared he might go to seed.

He told me that the members of his family did not make old bones. He reckoned that he had at the most ten more years and that he was ready and anxious for one more challenge. I told him that there were two openings: an established city parish where it was largely a question of maintaining existing provision, or another which was an immense task involving widespread development and reorganisation.

The priest said quite simply "I'll take whichever one you'll find more difficult to fill". Then he added: "And now that I've taken a pig in a poke, you had better tell me where it is".

Some weeks later he set out for his new assignment. He worked in the only way he knew: very hard and with thought only for his people. In the succeeding years he led them to new heights which had seemed almost unattainable. He carried through the reorganisation and prepared detailed plans for the future. With it all he offered a splendid home life in the presbytery he shared with the other priests and he was tireless in trying to meet the pastoral needs of his people.

He died in the way he had expected but a little earlier than he had expected. He had needed only half the ten years he had set himself. The genuine sorrow and mourning of his people were made supportable only by their joy and hope in the faith he had helped to build up amongst them. I doubt if he thought of himself as being expendable. It was just that, without imprudence, he felt incapable of giving to his people less than he had or of bringing to his priesthood anything less than his full energy and zeal. To his commitment to Christ there were attached no strings.

Even here there is a danger of over-simplification. In this condensed form it all sounds plain sailing: as if you set a target and then press on regardless, full steam ahead. In the constantly changing times in which we live it cannot be like that. Our aim is Christ. Our methods in reaching him and bringing others with us have often to be re-assessed. This is what brings ups and downs to a man's priesthood. His life is seldom a success story. He has to come to terms with the fact that he will not always meet with success, no matter how hard he works. Christ prayed that his disciples would be holy, not that they would have worldly success. The priest has to come to terms with heart-breaks just the same as other men.

It is in this context that his uncompromising commitment must be seen. It is the compassion which comes from a priest's sharing in Christ's suffering and rejection which determines that there can be no compromise in the measure in which he gives himself to Christ's work.

Someone was once discussing a priest with me. This priest was enormously talented, immensely popular, energetic and successful. In the eyes of the world he was certainly destined for "higher things". Then my friend made a very telling comment which explained a certain lack in this other priest's make-up which I had not been able to pin-point. "There is only one thing", he said. "He has not yet broken his heart like some others have. So he lacks compassion".

Compassion is often a wrongly-used word. It means "suffering with". In the case of a priest it means sharing in the passion of Christ and for this reason having practical sympathy with the sufferings and aspirations of his people.

This is what will lift him up and bring him down to earth. It is also what in the end will bear him down. For the more he feels with his people the less room can be left for him to consider himself.

It is at that time and in that sense that he becomes expendable: not as a result of a strategic exercise on a bishop's desk but in the Christ-like manner in which he gives himself to those for whom his Saviour died.

A priest is to the world a sign of Christ's suffering, death and resurrection. In some way he has to try to hold heaven and earth together. As he hangs on to both, his arms will be stretched out as were the arms of Jesus on Calvary. He will feel what has been called the "cross-pull". If he can with God's grace accept it, then he will know that the blood, sweat and tears of his priesthood are the strength on which the halt, the deaf and the blind, who are his charge, will live and hope on for that day when Christ will come again.

Compassion is bred of sharing in the passion of Christ whose promises demand from a priest a dedication which is uncompromising. Even then the priest knows that at times he will fail: no matter how hard he tries. He is not always bolstered by the company of his priestly brethren. Alone when smitten with the spiritually unaccountable, perhaps hurt beyond the understanding of others, he may easily fall victim to self-pity and to the depression which comes from stress. He can forget the cross which Christ has laid on him, the cross to which were nailed the feet washed by the tears of Magdalen's repentance. Confused and blinded by tears of pain rather than sorrow he can for a time lose sight of Christ and lose his bearings.

It is perhaps unlikely that the devoted priest will fall victim to the contemporary temptation of those who proclaim in self-defence that God is dead. But he will at times be beset by those who unrepentant seek in the name of conscience to justify their waywardness. He will be saddened but he must not be deterred by those who reject the ways which Christ has decreed for those he has chosen as his priests.

The way of repentance is the path to holiness to which Christ has called his priests. To rediscover Christ when we have strayed often requires the courage to lose someone or something else with which we have replaced him. To the priest who perseveres in faith and repentance, who accepts the suffering of compassion and the demands of commitment, who recognises the wounds of Christ in himself and in his people, is it too fanciful to believe that Christ speaks those words he once addressed to Thomas his disciple: "Give me your hand"?

THE PRIEST AND RENEWAL

At the close of the final session of the Council, Pope Paul recalled the words of his predecessor, who in the opening address had stated: "The greatest concern of this Ecumenical Council is this: that the sacred deposit of Christian doctrine be guarded and taught more effectively". But the present Holy Father went on to point out that, in the consideration of its mission, the Church in Council had also given itself to an unprecedented study of the modern world. "Never before", he said, "has the Church felt the need to know, to draw near to, to understand, to penetrate, serve and evangelise the society in which she lives; and to get to grips with it, almost to run after it, in its rapid and continuous change".

This, added the Pope, had already led to the suspicion that the Council had given way to "an easy-going and excessive responsiveness to the outside world, to passing events, cultural fashions, temporary needs, and an alien way of thinking". He thought these imputations false. Charity had been the principal religious feature of the Council, the ultimate meaning of which could be summed up as a "pressing and friendly invitation to mankind of today to rediscover God in fraternal charity".

It is perhaps as well to recall these words if we are looking at the renewal of the Church in which the priest

55

must fulfil his role. They indicate the new ground which has to be broken, the danger of confusion and the charity with which we must discover the means by which the sacred deposit of Christian faith is to be presented more effectively to the contemporary world. It is a doctrinal matter because we are dealing with the teachings of Jesus Christ. But it is no mere matter of academic theology, because we are dealing also with the setting of the world in which Christ's Church is incarnate.

Similarly with the priesthood: the issue today is not merely the theological problem of the priestly ministry; it is also — and in my experience much more frequently — the problem of the manner in which the priesthood is to be exercised in the world today. Put more crudely, it is often the problem of how the priest is being asked (or imagines that he is being asked) to live and exercise his priesthood in circumstances which to him seem unrelated to the spirit of renewal for which the Church has called.

Regarded by itself, the advice given in the Decree on Ecumenism seems straightforward enough: "Every renewal of the Church essentially consists in an increase of fidelity to her own calling" (art. 6).

But this renewal of the Church involves, as we have seen from the words of Pope Paul, "the penetration, service and evangelisation" of modern society. It is the task of the Church to bathe the world in the light of the Gospel but conversely members of the Church are deeply affected by what is happening in the world: by the changing structures in secular society, by contemporary needs and experience. Whilst the Church calls for renewal, the younger generation tells us openly that the choice is no longer between renewal and reform, but between reform and revolution.

Without experiencing the process of re-education and renewal which overtook most bishops in the Church during the Council, the young enthusiasts of today without further thought dismiss many of the subsequent reforms in the Church as utterly irrelevant to man's needs as they see them. At the present time society is concerned with its sickness, with the relief of suffering and injustice and poverty. We may speak of the dangers of humanism but we cannot ignore the background against which the renewal of the Church has to take place and in which she must be involved.

It is true that the priest cannot evangelise the world without first evangelising himself and the whole manner of his ministry. But, however spiritual a man may be, he will not achieve the renewal of his priestly role in a vacuum.

"The ministry of priests takes its start from the Gospel message and derives its power and force from the sacrifice of Christ" (*Presbyterorum Ordinis*, 2). "By the power of the sacrament of orders and in the image of Christ the Eternal High Priest, they are consecrated to preach the Gospel, shepherd the faithful and celebrate the divine worship as true priests of the New Testament" (*Lumen Gentium*, 28).

Many priests today, especially those who are genuinely concerned with the renewal of the Church, are highly sensitive about the image of the priesthood, seen not directly in the light of the Gospel but in the light of response to the needs of other men. They are anxious that their image should reflect that of Christ the servant. They insist that their life and ministry, seen against the background of man's condition here on earth, should be related to the service of mankind. They contend that in this they are answering the call to proclaim the word of God in a way that the world can understand that this is a necessary preliminary to calling the people together for worship.

The emphasis laid by the Council on the proclamation of the Word was not primarily a plea for better clerical enunciation, good ecclesiastical acoustics and for the use of modern mass media. The more effective and Christ-like proclamation of the word of God must be related to the very manner of existence of the priest.

Can he, given his present circumstances and the circumstances of those he must serve, evangelise the world by word and by example? Can he, by his whole life and ministry, show forth the full measure of Christ's love, sacrifice and mediation for men? The situation may very

E

well vary from one part of the world to another, but in my experience that is both the challenge and the difficulty facing the priest today.

There must be courageous and responsible experimentation, not just in pastoral techniques, but in the way in which the priest is to present the Gospel message and shepherd his flock. That is the challenge. If in his pastoral care he is to show the face of Christ to the world, the whole manner of his life must be Christ-like. That frequently is his difficulty. Where the conditions of his ministry seem to frustrate his giving of this patent witness, as he himself sees it to be needed, at best the priest feels personally unfulfilled, at worst he is apt to develop what he calls the crisis of his identity.

We know the need today for spiritual and rugged priests, but we must avoid the generalised condemnation of the frustrated and confused as victims of heresy, laxity or lust. If the priest is to play his part in the renewal of the Church, the manner of his life, his standard of living and his proclamation of the Gospel must have a realistic relationship to the needs, interests, conditions and aspirations of the world in which he must try to bring the love and service of Jesus Christ.

Circumstances vary so greatly from country to country that it would be pointless to do more than indicate briefly some of the spheres in which this principle of relevance must be applied. The priest's circumstances must be such that they contribute to his responsible and worthy proclamation of the Gospel, by word and by the example of his life. In addition to his personal holiness, he must be close to the people to whom he is to minister, not in a paternalistic way but close in sympathy and understanding, living a life which is in tune with the circumstances of their lives.

Mindful of his sublime office and of his priestly formation, we are apt to emphasise his personal dignity, as a priest. But his standard of living, his house, his meals, even his leisure, should not be an affront to the standards and dignity of those he is to serve. In the happiest parish of which I have had experience, the people claimed proudly that they had priests who "really cared".

A priest must be able to give expression to his "care" for those he is to shepherd in both their sorrows and their joys. Overmuch preoccupation with low-level administrative chores can dry up a priest's enthusiasm so that he seeks other opportunities for service. It is essential that no priest, whatever his place in the hierarchical structure of clerical life, should ever be left to feel that he has no responsibility in the exercise of his ministry and in the parish or institute in which he serves. Recently a young priest said: "If it is sometimes true that power corrupts and that absolute power corrupts absolutely, it is always true that lack of responsibility corrupts and total lack of responsibility corrupts absolutely".

This search for fulfilment in a ministry that is directed to the evangelisation of the world through service to mankind has given rise to much debate about the role of a priest. "Priests, through the ministry of bishops, are consecrated by God to become in a special way sharers of Christ's priesthood and his ministers in celebrating the sacred mysteries" (*Presbyterorum Ordinis*, 5).

In spite of the plethora of rubrical changes, the liturgical role of the priest seems clear enough. The problem for many seems to be how to reconcile this with what the priest is frequently asked to do outside his strictly liturgical function. In support of their contention that much of this work is unpriestly, they place emphasis on the distinction between his sacral and his non-sacral role. In my experience this distinction has often added to the confusion.

Academically real, it proves to be an unrealistic basis of separating activities which are frequently an extension one of the other. Indeed, I would argue that many of the duties of a priest now alleged to be "unpriestly" are in fact an extension of what is at the heart of the priesthood, viz., the proclamation of the word and the administration of the sacraments.

In claiming this I have not in mind such different

chores as duplicating the parish football pool results, cleaning the parish priest's car, or acting as telephonist or stenographer in the diocesan chancery. Even these can be works of service and of charity. But I am referring to such things as the care of the aged and the instruction of the young, the housing of the socially inadequate family, the counselling of parties to a matrimonial dispute, and the provision for the drug-addict and spirit-drinker. All would agree that these are good works but it is often alleged that they have nothing to do with the priestly ministry.

There are two further stages to this dangerous argument: first, that these tasks are better carried out by professional social and welfare workers, psychiatrists, trained marriage counsellors, and catechetical experts; and, second, that given the present state of society, all priests worth their salt and frustrated by time-wasting chores, would give better "Christian service" if they were to abandon their priesthood and seek training to enable them to act with true professional competence. This is the so-called crisis of confidence in the professional competence of the priest and is another affliction of good men genuinely desiring to play their part in the renewal of the Church.

If we are to overcome this apparent dichotomy, we must try to understand the relationship between what the priest does at the altar and what he is called upon to do to serve mankind. In this connection Karl Rahner writes:

"It is not that the man who performs the cult just happens to be pastor of souls as well. He is a pastor of souls *because* he performs the cult . . . because he is the man who makes present the reality of Christ, which is the beginning of the transfiguration of the world . . . Precisely because he is the man who performs the cult, the priest can never abandon what is his duty: that this earth should become totally redeemed, sanctified, justified — the kingdom of God.

"However much it is the authority and the duties he has in liturgical matters that are the beginning and the end for the priest, it is nevertheless what arises from these — the apostolic, prophetical, pastoral aspect of his vocation — that is the essentially determining factor in his life: the thing that sets a special stamp on his Christian life, differentiating it essentially from the life of the layman . . . A priest, then, is both a sacrificing priest and a pastoral priest in an interior, radical unity which involves both tasks in such fashion that neither can be truly fulfilled except in a mutual interpenetration" (*Mission and Grace*, vol. 2, ch. 2).

It seems essential that we understand this interpenetration, if we are not to be misled by an unrealistic separation of the priest's sacral role from his non-sacral role.

To care for the spiritual and material hunger of the people is surely a legitimate extension of the priest's eucharistic role. To teach may surely be seen as a means of preparing Christians to fulfil the obligations that are theirs from baptism. To give counsel in marriage may surely be seen as an extension of the priest's role in blessing a marriage contract. To assist in the settlement of disputes, personal, social or industrial, is but an extension of the priest's role in the sacrament of penance. To help the aged and to visit hospitals is clearly related to the administration of the sacrament of the sick.

When a priest is told that these tasks are better carried out by trained social welfare workers, probation officers, psychiatrists, etc., he should remember that Christ washed the feet of his disciples, he did not leave it to a skilled maidservant.

In a parish where once I served, a young mother presented herself at the priests' house to ask one of the curates to tell her husband when he returned from work that she had taken her children away and left him. The curate took her back to her home, which was in a chaotic condition; he made her sit down whilst he scrubbed the room, washed, clothed and fed the children. Then he left her to await the husband's return. Their reconciliation was not only to one another but to Christ.

Possibly a trained social welfare worker would have made a better job of the scrubbing and the cooking, but I believe that the achievement was due to the fact that it was a priest who had done it: because they knew it was the man who stood at the altar, that he was, in the words of Rahner, "the cult-man".

There is, of course, a danger here of over-simplification. It would be wrong to imagine that a knowledge of the rubrics, the sacramentary and the spiritual Fathers is enough. I would not wish to suggest that the priest today requires no other skills. Because a priest exercises his ministry in the world, he must endeavour to acquire additional technical competence in matters of concern to his people. He must try to understand their problems and achieve skill and experience which may be of value in easing these problems. But even when he has done this, he must remember that in their needs his people will approach him not primarily because of his technical competence but because he is a priest, their means of sacramental contact with Christ.

May I give a further example. Twice I have been called upon to advise in the settlement of major industrial disputes. Once the approach came from the Communist officials of a trade union engaged in a national strike. On the other occasion it was from Catholic stevedores in a dock strike. I have no doubt at all that on each occasion the approach was made to me because I was a priest, who could be presumed to be concerned about social justice, not because I was an industrial expert who happened to be a priest. Let a priest who is suffering from lack of confidence in his professional competence remember that his primary competence is that of the sacrificing priest with a pastoral concern. Herein lies his role in the renewal of his people.

My final point must deal with his personal sanctification, without which no priest can contribute to the renewal of the Church. If he is not to be under impossible tension, the spirituality of the priest must bear relation to his role of sharing in the mediation of Christ, of being the point of contact between God and man.

Points of contact can be "flash-points" caused by friction: an uncomfortable experience. Somehow the priest, increasingly involved in trying to meet the demands of those he serves, must achieve a relationship between his spiritual life and his ministry in the world. If he fails, he will surely break down. If he seeks merely to achieve a compromise, he will satisfy neither God nor man. Somehow he must relate his personal spirituality to his service of the community: and let us not pretend that these are identical. "Priests cannot be ministers of Christ unless they are witnesses and dispensers of a life other than this earthly one. But they cannot be of service to men if they remain strangers to the life and condition of men" (*Presbyterorum Ordinis,* 3).

Priests are men of the Church. Their relationship with God is through the Church in which the Spirit of God is breathing. They are made what they are by the Church, nurtured and sustained by her. She forms their modes of worship and their life of prayer. So if we are at this time seeking new insights into the Church of Christ, we should not be surprised that these changes and developments are reflected in the opportunities sought and the difficulties experienced by a priest in his efforts to live his life of prayer.

One of the principal dangers would seem to be that, in his search for relevance in his ministry and witness, the priest may not only reject as irrelevant many of the spiritual maxims and methods which have served earlier generations but he may replace them with nothing else. The imagery of the Psalter may prove uninspiring to some young men. But what is much more worrying is their failure to search for an alternative: irrelevance is not best countered by the mere achievement of extra time for relaxation.

The renewal of the Church will not be achieved solely by greater efficiency or by more acceptable pastoral techniques. The basic problem facing many priests today is the intensification of their spirituality in face of the constantly growing demands for activity in service of their people. It is easy to say that they must "get their priorities right". But it is my belief that, just as in the pastoral needs of the people priests must pool their resources and talents and work together in meeting the complex challenge of modern society, so in spiritual matters priests must also pool their resources and endeavour to assist one another, not just on community worship, but in the intensification of their personal spirituality.

The priest who really commits himself to the renewal of the Church today becomes subject to immense pressures, physical, psychological and spiritual. Under such pressures he may possibly be tempted to abandon the Vatican Council's commitment of the Church to the service of mankind and to imitate the isolation of St Simon Stylites. One thing is certain: he cannot face these challenges and difficulties alone.

"Priests are intimately united in a sacramental brother-hood . . . Each priest is united to his brethren in the bonds of love, prayer and complete co-operation. They should be genuinely helpful to each other and ready to share what they possess" (*Presbyterorum Ordinis*, 8). Possibly because of their preoccupation with their role in the communal worship of their people, priests have in my experience seldom faced up to their need to help one another in their personal spirituality.

So great is the concentration upon the reorganisation and redeployment of priests for their more effective pastoral ministry that inadequate attention is given to sharing spiritual possessions. Thought has to be given to achieving the best means whereby priests may sustain one another in the new spiritual needs arising from their all-consuming commitment in the service of the Church as she endeavours to renew herself in her "renewal of the face of the earth".

Some years ago, shortly before the end of the Council, I spent all day with the team of priests whom I was leading at that time in the East End of London. It was an early experiment at renewal. As frankly as possible we discussed our lives, methods and activities in the parish church, in the parish itself and in the presbytery where we lived together. Towards the end of the day the youngest priest present hit the table with his fist and exploded with expletives I cannot here repeat. How could we effectively work together, he asked, if we did not pray together?

It had taken us eigtheen months to reach this realisation. We had learned to live as a family. We had learned to share the use of our possessions. We had learned to share our talents, such as they were, to act responsibly in the name of the Church and to keep one another informed of individual activities. We shared the lessons of our reading of assigned literature. We met regularly with priests of neighbouring areas to share experience of the priesthood in a changing society in which we were trying to turn our parishes into outward-looking worshipping communities with a Christian social purpose. Yet somehow something was still missing. Then it became apparent. We needed to share our spirituality. We needed to pray together.

But here I would merely wish to emphasise that the value of all these things is limited if there is no bond of prayer between the priests themselves. Priests engaged in the renewal of the Church must break through the "prayer-barrier" if their natural camaraderie is to be uplifted to the spiritual brotherhood of the priestly order.

We are members of a pilgrim Church, whose mission from Christ remains the same in a changing society. The manner in which priests will exercise their ministry in the Church may well change, rubrically in their liturgical function and more radically in the calls made upon them outside the liturgy.

Renewal for priests consists essentially in an intensification of fidelity to their calling. Always they are at heart the cult-men and to them the pilgrim Church gives their marching orders: "Let them, as fathers in Christ, take care of the faithful whom they have begotten by baptism and by their teaching. Having become from the heart a pattern to the flock, let them so lead and serve their local community that it may worthily be called by that name by which the one and entire people of God is distinguished: namely, the Church of God" (*Lumen Gentium*, 28).

GROUP MINISTRY OR TEAM-WORK

In these days of participation "team-work" has become a vogue word to denote something with near magical qualities. Yet in the setting of the Church the basic notion is that of sharing: sharing of responsibility for a particular task or area, and sharing whatever resources or talents, intellectual, physical and material, may be available for that task or area. It would be a great mistake to imagine that this necessarily means the bringing together in one house of a group of specialists who are going to revolutionise a district with new techniques — or a group of inadequates who are going to find in companionship and planned living an answer to the demands of celibacy or a salve to their frustrations and isolation. There can be many variations in the form of group ministry but the basic idea is to pool resources for the better pastoral care of others. It may also be advantageous to the spirituality and living standards of the priests concerned, thereby helping them to work better. But that is not the direct principal purpose of group ministry, which is designed for the more effective service of the people.

If we accept this basic concept, it follows that there can be almost as many variations in the form group ministry can take as there are different situations to be met. It is possible for a number of priests, living together in one house and serving one parish, to operate a group ministry. This is why people sometimes say that there is no difference between team-work and the ideal parish set-up as they claim to have known it. In fact it is unlikely that any one presbytery can contain all the talents required to meet the needs of any one parish.

Neighbouring parishes may often share some problems: almost certainly they need to share also the particular qualities and experience to be found in the neighbouring parishes. It is not merely the complications of a technological age that make it difficult, sometimes impossible and almost always undesirable, for the priest of a parish to "go it alone". A simple example is that of a priest of a parish who has been trained to teach modern catechetical methods: it is likely that all the schools in the area need his services, not just the school in the parish to which he happens to be appointed. The same can be said of a priest with genuine aptitude for youth service, social welfare work, even work with specialised professional groups.

In many places this kind of sharing of talents already takes place, though its full benefits are often diminished by too much consciousness of parish boundaries, rights, not "poaching", etc. How often is the work of a school chaplain impeded by his not being able to visit the home and parents of problem children living in other parishes? Similarly children attending the same school but coming from different parishes are submitted to varying sacramental disciplines because of the lack of a common policy between neighbouring parishes. Consultation to achieve such elementary cooperation for the benefit of the people is an example of group ministry or team-work in its simplest form.

A slightly more elaborate group ministry, which could be fairly generally applicable, can be the deanery, provided that the dean himself enjoys the confidence of his brethren, and such authority (delegated by the Ordinary) as is compatible with his genuine leadership. Another condition is normally that the deanery be compact enough for its component parishes and priests to share many similar problems, to enjoy ease of communication and to be able to give effective mutual help. To some extent this form of team-work is already in practice, with priests of a deanery agreeing that the specialised works of the deanery be carried out by those of the brethren who have the time and aptitude to perform them.

All this is obviously possible with a group of city parishes, only a mile or two apart. It must be realised that it can be just as valuable in a group of rural parishes ("one-horse" missions) where the isolation of individuals with inadequate equipment to meet all the needs of their people can be changed into inter-dependence with mutual help, an inter-change of talents and a coordination of the Church's mission in the entire area. For this there must be real leadership by the dean, exercising a certain pastoral responsibility for all the parishes in the deanery and for the welfare of the other priests. Inevitably there have also to be regular meetings to exchange information and formulate policy. This frequently leads to a more effective service of the people of the entire area and also to a notable increase in the morale of the priests, otherwise frustrated by the limitations of their isolation.

If this idea is taken a stage further, it may sometimes be desirable to combine all these small units in a single deanery-parish, with most if not all the priests living together and operating from one base. For this to be pastorally effective local circumstances must be taken into consideration. From point of view of the priests, there must be a good leader for the team and a reasonable balance and congeniality amongst the members. From point of view of the people it is essential that they should know when and where to find the priest responsible for their area (e.g. on the consulting room basis where the priest endeavours to keep "surgery hours"); even more important the priest should not be housed so far away that the people no longer feel that he belongs to them. The distance is obviously relative in both town and country: as a factor in determining the size of the group ministry it cannot be over-emphasised. But there is no reason why there should not be "living-out" members to a team, provided that they maintain close contact with those at the base-presbytery and are to some extent under the direction of the leader.

What are the advantages of such coordination? So far as the people are concerned it usually leads to better pastoral care, based on a wider experience, the use of additional talents from other members of the team, often a marked financial economy and the service of a priest who is looked after properly and sustained by the brotherhood of those with whom he is living.

How does it work out in practice? Experience suggests that the joint responsibility of the team for the whole area is best shown by the leader, who has special responsibility for the church to which the base presbitery is attached, making a point of offering Mass at each out-station on successive Sundays and, being spared a normal district for visiting, making a point of visiting families all over the area, especially the sick, new-comers and problem families to whom the other priests call his attention. Each of the other priests has a special, though not exclusive, responsibility for a district of the whole area covered by the team. He will normally celebrate Mass in that area, possibly neighbourhood or house-Masses on weekdays, and in the out-station on Sundays (save when the team leader is present). He will arrange to be at some centre in his district at a certain time each day so that the people know that they can find him there; the publication of the place of house-Masses will also help in this. He will normally be responsible for servicing any institutions in his district, unless it falls in some special category for which another member of the team has responsibility. But clearly if a sick person from one district enters hospital in another, he will be cared for by the priest responsible for the hospital but visited by the priest from the area where he normally resides.

Pastoral visitation of the homes will normally be reported to all members of the team, and the streets, etc., to be visited will be advertised throughout the whole territory.

Special projects in the territory will normally be planned in common and, if they call for help, be supported by all the priests. The unity of the team must be seen and understood by the people. It is best exemplified by concelebration of Mass regularly at the base church and in the out-stations on special occasions, e.g. patronal feasts. Exchange of pulpits and confessors is easily arranged. But for a group of priests to be seen as a real brotherhood or team by the people, it is essential that there be loyalty and a regular exchange of information between them.

The special responsibility of the individual members of a team is not restricted to districts but also covers spheres of specialised activity. Individuals may be appointed to have responsibility for chaplaincies to schools, to hospitals and even to care for old people: priests often have these special aptitudes. Similarly members can take on special responsibility for the youth work, particular problems of social welfare, the organisation of instruction classes, etc. By the allocation of these special responsibilities it is possible for all the priests to organise their working hours better, reduce the danger of duplication and ensure that the best man for the particular job is employed. But if the danger of independent action by those who merely happen to be living in the same house is to be overcome, there must be regular sessions for reporting and consultation. It is not unusual that laymen also are drawn in a special way to the work undertaken by the priests. There is no reason why, as their commitment is proven, they should not be admitted as a lay echelon to the team, sharing in at least some of the consultation. They often blossom under this treatment and have a real contribution to make. Nuns also can make a most effective contribution to the work of a team, especially if trained as teachers, social workers or in youth and community service.

In saying that ideally the members of a team live together as a family, with proper regard for one another's needs and temperaments, one cannot stress too strongly the importance of the role of the leader. He does not have to be a forceful character but he does have to weld the others together and lead them in their spiritual commitment as well as being their chairman or managing director. Experience suggests that whereas there is sometimes gain to be had from gathering into a team priests of similar temperament and ideals, the leader must have some clear seniority in age or experience so that, even if he is not a father figure, he is at least "big brother". Current suggestions that a team should be a democratic unit, with the role of president passing from one member to another at regular intervals, have already been shown to be impractical for the priests and pastorally unsound for the people. In any case the members of a new team take at least a year to grow together.

Great importance is to be attached to the members sharing all that they have, within reason. Ideally there must be common use of such things as cars, books, etc. Truly in this way will a real family spirit be created. But this sharing should also be related to matters spiritual. Obviously in public worship they should all try to follow the same customs, ideally the same line when preaching, etc., but if at all possible they should help each other with personal spiritual development. By this is meant not just personal counselling, but discussing together thoughts for homilies, spiritual reading and periodicals, and, most important and most difficult of all, praying together, e.g. some of the Divine Office together each day. There is no better way of uniting men or of easing the tensions which will inevitably arise from time to time between over-enthusiastic members of a team. Home-life would seem also to imply the existence of a common living-room, used as any family would use it, and a real effort by all members to make sure that they are all at home together at least one evening in the week. By supplying each other's spiritual and human needs in this way, even at the loss of traditional individual privacy, the members of a household become a real team, sharing a real group ministry.

So far I have dealt merely with teams of priests operating

within the traditional parish or deanery structure and serving the general needs of a particular area. But use can also be made of teams to meet the special needs of a parish or group of parishes, needs which are normally beyond the competence of the parish priest or curate in whose territory this situation, calling for specialised training or experience, may arise. A team of several priests may be used to meet one extensive need, e.g. an industrial team, dealing with ministry to those in industry who have lapsed or lack contact with Church or clergy. Or there can be a team of priests whose tasks comprise a number of specialised works calling for special training and possibly tasks which because they are inter-parochial are everybody's and nobody's responsibility.

It will be seen that such teams differ from those previously mentioned in that they are extra-parochial or, perhaps better, inter-parochial, serving all parishes but without any normal commitment to one particular parish. On the other hand it is vital that such a team of specialists be fully integrated into the local presbyterium, ideally being answerable through their leader to the local dean. This team must be seen as complementary to the parish clergy and not as an alternative or replacement. For obvious reasons it is often desirable to secure the understanding and cooperation of the local clergy by ensuring that the team be led by a secular priest or at least a suitable priest chosen by or acceptable to all the parishes whose special needs are to be served by the team. There is no reason at all why the members of such a team should not be religious: indeed often this is a way for religious to return to the kind of work for which they were founded, to be integrated in a pastoral ministry and yet be able to achieve some form of communal life. Experience suggests that this may be of increasing importance to the smaller congregations whose young men are often impatient for pastoral work: it has already been shown that without conflict of interest such a specialised team can comprise both seculars and regulars including members from different congregations.

F

In such a specialised group ministry the over-riding consideration should be the local need. It is not a case of collecting specialists (or misfits) and seeing how their talents can be employed. First, local needs must be assessed. Then priests must be found who have the qualifications to meet those needs or, in their absence, first class men must be trained to meet the actual needs that exist. These members must be fit for membership of a team which will have to provide professional or competent skill to do a job for which the parish clergy have neither the time nor the aptitude. In such a team the principles of special responsibility, as already explained, apply. But frequently, when there is a specially increased demand, the other members of the team will be able to help as a body. The sustaining of a man under strain is another obvious advantage. In addition to individual special responsibilities, there are therefore also shared responsibilities, which will mean that regular reporting between members is even more important. Apart from these specialised tasks, e.g. chaplaincy to a college of education, a large comprehensive school, a seaport, coloured immigrants, some special field of social welfare, etc., other uses for such a team are tasks which are inter-parochial and difficult for any one person to tackle, e.g. the training of catechists, the provision of religious instruction on a Saturday for Catholic children in non-Catholic secondary schools, etc. As a rule, the main danger for such a team of competent enthusiasts is that they are apt to collect too soon too many tasks for them to absorb. But here again experience shows that good laity and sisters often offer help to a team of this kind and can become an effective echelon, sharing many works with the priests who, by bringing them ever more fully into consultation, are able to give formation to valuable leaders.

It is still arguable as to whether such a team should be based on a church. In certain circumstances it could be valuable, even if only so that the other priests do not regard members of a team as a race apart. But it can often diminish their usefulness to other parishes, it can lessen amongst all the parishes the sense of sharing the benefits of the team and it can also create rivalries with neighbouring churches. There is the further point that the members must normally be free of a church commitment if they are to take the Mass and the sacraments to the specialised areas which they are serving.

All that I have already written about the need for leadership and a spiritual brotherhood amongst the members applies most strongly in a specialised team of this kind. It goes without saying that it is of special importance in the case of a team working in an industrial or predominantly secular field. It can only be entrusted to first-class men. The great danger is that such work appeals (in theory) to misfits. It is interesting that many of the principles set out above apply equally to the small communities of three or four nuns now being established in new estates, etc., to give service to the special needs of such an area.

One last important point: finance. The best principle is that each team must be financially viable. In the kind of parish team or deanery-parish team I have mentioned, economy is usually affected, especially where several small presbyteries are abandoned in favour of one parish-house. (One must try to avoid creating a large institution, immediately putting the priests in a different social category from those they are to serve). In specialised teams finance must be pooled: at least half the numbers will need to be bread-winners, doing work carrying salaries or entitled to grants. Most families of five have at least two bread-winners: a specialised team must have the same. This is important in selecting the works to be entrusted to the team concerned. But the pooling of finance amongst several established parishes is always the crunch-point and can seldom be achieved at once.

Group ministry calls for really good priests, especially in experimental days. Such groups often require the closest link with the local bishop as well as the local clergy: he will have to attend some of their consultations, advise and sustain. Perhaps his hardest problems will be to secure the acceptance of the idea in advance by the other clergy, to convince the laity that this scheme is to help the parochial system and not to replace it and to shield such teams from the glamour and publicity to which mass media will wish to treat them, often rendering their work impossible by floodlighting their experimental footsteps just when they do not wish to be seen.

At explanatory meetings it may well be argued that the Church is replacing the general practitioner with a group medical service, or the local constable with "Panda-Car" police. There is this difference. The doctor does not call to leave behind him medical auxiliaries, nor the policeman to establish special constables. Priests working in a group ministry will be well equipped to help form those they visit to serve in the apostolate of their own area.

THE DIACONATE:
A RESTORED MINISTRY WITH A FUTURE

All the faithful derive their responsibility in the life of the Church from the fact of their baptism. Yet it is probably true to say that clericalism is more likely to die because of their not being enough priests to go round than because of the sudden enlightenment of the masses about the true role of the laity. I have often wondered whether the present shortage of vocations to the priesthood and to the religious life — at least in some parts of the world — is not the Lord's way of making sure that the layman is given his rightful opportunities in the parish where he lives.

Without trying to be too much of a prophet, I will at least venture the belief that as the laity discover their full responsibilities, so the family-life in the Church will improve. Families will see better the tasks facing the Church, the different roles and vocations to be filled, and they may even begin to look amongst their own members to see who should undertake which particular responsibility. If we get lay life right now, there may be more missionary priests, teaching brothers and contemplative religious in the future.

There is another aspect of this matter where I will more readily assume the mantle of a prophet. One of the key characters in the Church of the future will be the deacon. It may well happen in the first place because dioceses will be looking for men to distribute the Eucharist and to lead communities in worship in those areas where there are no longer priests or enough priests to maintain past services. But in fact the restoration of the permanent diaconate in the Church is a great embellishment in the whole pattern of service given by the Church to the community.

We are discovering wonderful new opportunities where genuine ministry can be exercised in bringing God's word into circumstances which in the past were often closed or unexplored. Men are emerging from our parishes who, with the grace of Holy Orders, are able to exercise this real ministry in a manner and in spheres which must in all honesty be called "new ground".

The diaconate is a real ministry in itself and not just a probationary state for those approaching priestly ordination. It is the first degree of the triple order of the ordained ministry — diaconate, priesthood and episcopate. It is a distinct ministry and should not be seen as a consolation prize for those who cannot, because of matrimonial bond or lack of education, make the next grade, the priesthood.

It is often easier to describe what a person does than to define what he is. This is true of a deacon as it is also true of a layman. Of deacons the Constitution *Lumen Gentium* speaks this way: "Strengthened by sacramental grace they are dedicated to the people of God, in conjunction with the bishop and his body of priests, in their service of the liturgy, of the Gospel and of works of charity" (art. 19). We speak much of service with regard to the diaconate but we should be careful not to limit thereby our idea of the scope of the deacon's work.

The ordination rite tells us that deacons are to preach and teach the Gospel. They are to assist priests in liturgical worship and in the sacrifice of the Mass. They are "to instruct the faithful in doctrine, preside over public prayer, confer baptism, assist at marriages, bring viaticum to the dying and lead the rites of burial". As ministers of charity they are to attend to the material as well as to the spiritual needs of the faithful.

When some years after the Council the decree restoring the diaconate laid much emphasis on the liturgical and sacramental side of the deacon's work, there were many who wrongly regarded the diaconal ministry as part-time work to be carried out at weekends and where there was a shortage of priests. This inevitably led to a conflict of views: what could a deacon do that a layman (especially an extra-ordinary minister of Holy Communion) was not already doing? This viewpoint was countered by those who argued equally strongly that someone who was to be entrusted with such work should not be deprived of the sacramental grace of Holy Orders.

It may help if I give some account here of the steps I took with regard to the preparations for the ordination of my first permanent deacon. He was a married man in his early forties, was a convener of a lay apostolic movement in the diocese and was used to working with priests as well as laity. He had a good job in a factory, a sensible wife and was generally held acceptable in the new town where he was living and where a group ministry of priests was operating. I had long talks with the group leader (or dean) who undertook to help this man with his studies under my general supervision. We decided on the general principle that a would-be deacon should normally be drawn from the local Church or parish, for training (if possible) by a priest or priests from the local Church, and for diaconal service in that local Church.

We worked out a scheme for training over a minimum of two years: training in dogmatic and moral theology, catechetics, holy scripture, and in counselling. Most of the early work was carried out by the candidate's reading in the evenings after he had completed his day's work. Each weekend he spent several hours with the parish priest who acted as his tutor and taught him to write essays and eventually homilies (which the future deacon used to try out on his wife). He came to see me quarterly so that I could check up on his progress and try to encourage him. I also saw his wife regularly to make sure that the man had her full understanding and support. In fact she tried to help him by being his audience and she also took a course in counselling to help any of those whom her husband might later refer to her.

The local clergy were very sensible in all this. Periodically they invited man and wife to presbytery meals and I made sure that they were invited whenever we gathered our candidates for the priesthood. In practice there was never the slightest difficulty where relationships were concerned. After a year of training the man was given his first convert to instruct and was sent out to give talks to ecumenical and parish groups. He also started his own Christian ethics group in his factory.

After this first candidate had received some eighteen months of training, I suggested that the parish priest gently and gradually let the other parishioners know about the man's proposed ordination to the diaconate. He started to serve in the sanctuary of the main church in the area and, after he had received the first ministry of lector, he read regularly at Mass. When he had received the second ministry he began to help with the distribution of Holy Communion but he did not preach until he had received the diaconate. The people took all this in their stride.

The ordination in the parish church, packed out with enthusiastic parishioners and with the man's friends and family, was a particularly happy day. I had been anxious about his wife's feelings: she assured me that her happiness that day ranked with her wedding-day and she felt that her husband's diaconate had given an added meaning to the bond of love between them and the support she must give him in his new ministry.

My major difficulty has been to overcome the idea that because this man goes to work he is to be thought of only as a "part-time" deacon. I have to emphasise the triple nature of his ministry. First, there is his work as a deacon in his factory where his diaconate has become known and where his Christian discussion group is only one aspect of his ministry — he is as frequently approached by those wanting his counsel on marriage as he is about social justice. There is also his ministry in his own home where, aided by his wife, he gives witness in marriage and family life lived in accordance with the Gospel he preaches and alongside those who share his married state as well as the task of going out to earn a living. Finally, there is his ministry in his parish where apart from certain liturgical duties at weekends, he supervises the parish apostolic groups, instructs converts and has an area of the new town, for which he is responsible for visiting, etc.

I treat of this example at length because there is already evidence of how much good has been achieved by what this permanent deacon has been able to do. It seems clear also that in many parishes in the future, where there is perhaps only one priest and much more than one priest can do in the preaching of the word, the administration of the sacraments and in the service of the flock, a permanent deacon of this calibre will not only be a help: it is really likely to be the only answer.

Two other features have emerged which I did not anticipate. Although the deacon to whom I have referred had already engaged in much apostolic work as a layman, his teaching has now proved much more effective and acceptable, not just because of the training he has received but because he is recognised as having the authority of Order in teaching the truths of his religion. The other factor we had not anticipated was the extent to which it has proved possible for a deacon to be a link between priests and lay parishioners. No priest likes to feel that such a link is necessary. But for some people it is an undoubted advantage to have a deacon who, precisely because he seems to have, as it were, a foot in both camps, is able to represent and interpret the lay parishioner to the priest and *vice versa*.

Not all permanent deacons work in the fashion I have indicated. Nor is it necessary for them strictly to be based on a parish, even though they must belong to a particular diocese. As I have said, new ground is being broken. There are already signs that the diaconate can be exercised effectively in spheres to which a "herald of the Gospel" has not easily been admitted in the past. Heraldry may be an ancient device but to be a herald means to bring a message to others in a way they can both hear and understand. To be heard one must be close. To be understood one must have the right language. The restored diaconate would seem to have an assured place in the renewed Church.

THE PASTORAL ROLE OF RELIGIOUS

I have already quoted that extract from the Decree on Ecumenism where we are told that "every renewal of the Church consists essentially in an increase of fidelity to her own calling". We shall get nowhere without this intensification in our faith and this means first and foremost an intensification in our spiritual life. The Church in Council demands greater dedication, not relaxation. This is particularly true in our spiritual practices. Because certain prayers and practices no longer attract and seem anachronistic, it is no use our just wiping them out of our life. We must replace them by something which does mean more to us.

Once, visiting a convent, I sat with the sisters who were telling me all about their changes. I am afraid that I could not fail to note that at first hearing these all appeared to be relaxations: we get up half an hour later, we can talk during meals, we can watch television, we can go out alone — the sort of things the junior novices used to be put up to ask the bishop when he came — a novena of long sleeps, recreations, tea-parties, etc. When I commented on the fact, one sister said: "Yes, but I feel so much better psychologically, so much more a person, a woman, that I can do my job in religion and in life better". It was a good point. She could be right: I hope she was. But let us be clear on one point. We shall not play our part adequately in the evangelisation of the world, our world, unless we first evangelise ourselves and see our role in this work in the context of the work and the life of the Church.

We should be wary of the "no time now" excuse as a result of greater commitment to the so-called "world". We can love people for their own sake, but in Christ. An essential part of building up our faith is to ask ourselves "Why" at regular intervals — and try to answer honestly and face up to the consequences. Just as it is important to know why we enter religion — love of Christ, not escape — so it is important to keep faith with him in our new opening up of work and daily life. In all this we should not forget to help one another, because in our inexperience we can be very vulnerable. But greater involvement in the work of the Church nearly always means a greater degree of sharing — even in the religious life.

For religious the first criterion in any shared work must be what is best for the people who are to be served. It is not a question of new openings for those who want to do their own things. A bishop is neither computer nor magician in coordinating the idiosyncrasies of those wishing to opt out of religious life. He is however responsible for trying to discern the genuine needs of his people and then seeing how best they can be met from *all* the resources available in the diocese — and sometimes elsewhere.

"A diocese", we are told, "is that portion of God's people which is entrusted to a bishop to be shepherded by him with the cooperation of the presbyterium. Adhering thus to its pastor and gathered together by him in the Holy Spirit through the Gospel and the Eucharist, this portion constitutes a particular Church in which the one, holy, catholic and apostolic Church of Christ is truly present and operative" (*Christus Dominus*, 11).

The same decree states that "All religious have the duty, each according to his proper vocation, of cooperating zealously and diligently in building up and increasing the whole Mystical Body of Christ and for the good of the particular Churches" (*Ibid.*, 33). In these quotations lie the strength and the weakness of collaboration between religious and the diocesan bishop and clergy. Clearly the apostolate in an area is essentially linked with the responsibility of the local or particular Church. On the other hand, religious, even in matters other than that of the internal order of their communities, sometimes find it difficult to commit themselves to an apostolate identified with the local Church.

The obstacle may be due to regular posting to houses in one diocese after another. It may be that the demands made of them have too little regard for those words "each according to his proper vocation". But even though the antipathies of the past have largely gone, the actual structural differences of membership of an Order, not necessarily tied to a particular religious house, and the allegiance and obedience of a diocesan priest to a particular Church (or diocese), still constitute a difficulty for all concerned. It may be due to changing religious superiors — bishops also come and go — or it may be due to obedience which takes a religious from one part of the country to another. The spirit of dioceses differ, especially today. But the lack of stability of religious committed to the pastoral mission in a diocese still presents a not inconsiderable difficulty when it comes to sharing in the mission of the local or particular Church.

If the first principle is "what is calculated to give the best service to the people of God", it follows that normally speaking the sharing by religious in the apostolic or pastoral mission of an area must be within the context of the local Church. Negatively, the area cannot be the trial ground for religious, individuals or a group, to make experiments for their personal hobby-horse. Positively if the mission of the Church — and we belong to the same Church and share the same mission — is to be credible and effective, then the apostolic and pastoral endeavour of religious in an area must be seen as part of that mission and must fit in with what others are doing with the authority of the bishop in the local Church.

85

It is impossible to list the very many ways in which religious can and do share mission in a diocese. The care of parishes is an established fact. I hope we are past the stage of thinking of this as just a good way of saving diocesan clergy, or of obtaining pastoral cover for difficult areas. But I must point to the advantage, especially in semi-rural parishes of countless villages or in newly developing estates, if religious will help in building up the parish and getting things started. Orders are often willing to take on places where the diocese would or could expend only one man. A little community of two or three can not only set such a parish on its feet but can also be a great help to surrounding "one-horse parishes" by giving help in carrying through a venture which one priest on his own could not attempt.

It would be dishonest not to mention snags. The biggest snag arises from enforced changes of personnel, parish priests and superiors, because of the requirements of holy rule or regulation. Secular priests and curates also change, but within the same diocese, the same local Church, and within much the same spirit. It can be a major disaster to a parish with a close bond between priest and people, and close collaboration within the parish council — always to be seen as chosen fellow-workers in the work of evangelisation — if the rule requires a move and there is an import from "foreign" parts, who may have nothing of the spirit of the diocese and may disapprove of parish councils. It takes a lot of explaining to the people who cannot believe that the replacement is not the bishop's personal choice. These changes are anxious times: they are often the reason why perhaps no one should assume care of a parish unless he has already served his apprenticeship in the diocese beforehand. It is only fair to all concerned.

It would seem to me not unlikely that in the future we shall see in the parish-structure of this country a development of the same two-tier system which will be in civil local government. There already exists a system of "related parishes", where neighbouring parishes, each with a priest responsible for its ordinary pastoral care, are grouped under a leader or dean who has overall responsibility for the whole area to ensure the provision of certain services to all the parishes — services which could not and need not be repeated in each parish. Where one of the parishes or even the lead-parish could be staffed by several religious, the provision of these supplementary services would be an obvious possibility.

I have written mostly of priests but there is increasing proof of successful sharing of pastoral care with religious brothers and sisters. I hope to see brothers more closely associated with group and team ministries. They could give immense help in the field of youth work and in the religious education of children in State schools in new towns and estates. There is no real reason why they should not be a complete unity within a group ministry, but it might be good for a community of school brothers to have a member or two able and willing to do catechetical or even probation work nearby. All I would ask is that it be within the context of the group or local Church.

As for the role of women religious, I cannot over-emphasise the importance of work which can be done for a parish by sisters in that parish. This is quite apart from the question of establishing small communities specifically for pastoral work. There are, of course, wonderful opportunities for these special communities of parish sisters.

The basic principle is once again the better service of the people. It may also be the chosen means of sanctification for the sisters but one thing is quite clear: it is doomed to failure if it is set up independently of the local Church, of the bishop and priests; or if it is seen as a means of finding an escape or outlet for sisters whose enthusiasms or eccentricities cannot be contained within the normal full community.

A small community of parish sisters should be established because of local needs, not because of the apparent necessity to set up small communities. However difficult it may be to contain the personality problems and demands of individuals in a large community, there will be no solution —

certainly without cost to the local parish — merely by trying to find a small round hole into which to place some irregular shaped "square" pegs — or *vice versa*.

The Second Vatican Council, with its insight into the nature and mission of the Church, successfully put an end to separate compartments in which bishops, priests, religious and laity try to play their part in the general response to Christ's call to follow him. New relationships have had to be established at every level and in every aspect of the Church's life and mission. This is not a betrayal of former ways and loyalties. It is seeing how we follow our different vocations together. It will be important that this is worked out in a practical manner in the local Church. No one has responded more generously and bravely to the Church's call to renewal than the religious — especially religious sisters. All ministries will need to collaborate if adaptation and renewal of religious life are to be given genuine pastoral expression in the local Church without loss of that religious identity which has been a true embellishment of the Church over the centuries.

THE LAYMAN IN THE CHURCH

When I am asked to talk about the lay apostolate and I emphasise "The Layman *IN* the Church", it is because I fear that it is not only my English accent which may land us with "The Layman *AND* the Church". That word "*IN*" is perhaps the most significant thing which happened to the Church in my life-time — and a very precious thing it is. For without burdening you with too much history, may I just say that for many centuries the layman was largely a "non-person", someone who had the misfortune not to be a priest. To some extent this — at least in the early centuries — reflected the make-up of society itself. But little had happened in the Church to keep pace with the growth in professional competence and responsibility of the ex-serf, now citizen. With the Second Vatican Council. that up-dating took place and the layman assumed his role and responsibilities as a full member of the Church, sharing responsibility for the mission entrusted by Christ to *all* his followers.

Relatively short memories will recall the process in more recent years, with the development of "Catholic Action" under Pius XI, where almost all lay activity worth its salt had to be carried out by direct mandate from the bishop or bishops and within highly structured diocesan organisations. In its manner of acting the Church often

G

reflects contemporary secular structures and we should not forget the highly organised and disciplined forms of national socialism prevalent at that time. With Pius XII, especially in the post-war years, the laity moved forward to the position of being "auxiliaries of the hierarchy".

The fundamental change came, of course, with the Second Vatican Council: not just in the Decree on the Apostolate of the Laity, but pre-eminently with the Constitution on the Church and especially with chapter II of the document which deals with the people of God. It is from this that the subsequent chapter on the laity, the Decree on the Lay Apostolate and, you might say, all Conciliar teaching with regard to the layman, flow. In this great decree is made clear that all the baptised share in the life and mission of the Church, that there is hierarchical order in the Church and there are different vocations and tasks to be fulfilled, but that between all ministries there is equality of dignity. The student may search in vain for such phrases as "auxiliaries of the hierarchy". Instead he will find in article 33 of the Constitution on the Church this definition of the lay apostolate:

"The lay apostolate is a participation in the saving mission of the Church itself. Through their baptism and confirmation, all are commissioned to that apostolate by the Lord himself. Moreover, through the sacraments, especially the Holy Eucharist, there is communicated and nourished that charity towards God and man which is the soul of the entire apostolate. Now, the laity are called in a special way to make the Church present and operative in those places and circumstances where only through them can she become the salt of the earth. Thus every layman, by virtue of the very gifts bestowed upon him, is at the same time a living witness and a living instrument of the mission of the Church herself".

And there it is. The task is there because of baptism and confirmation and not because of the shortage of priests or the eccentricity of an interested curate. The task is also there primarily in the secular sphere because that is where primarily and normally the layman operates. But the words which are of the greatest significance are "a living witness" and "a living instrument of the mission of the Church herself". Not auxiliary status, no half-measures; as a baptised Christian, the layman has his own particular task to carry out in the mission of the Church.

The Decree on the Lay Apostolate develops this theme of the various fields of the apostolate and singles out for mention the parish, the family, amongst young people, the social milieu and inevitably in national and international life. But in practice that all sounds at a fairly high and professional level — a job for the experts rather than for the masses. Today this is almost certainly the main problem. The gates have been opened — in most places, at least. The invitation (a favourite word with Pope Paul) has been issued — in most places, at least. And the response, amidst a great deal of goodwill on all sides — and in most places, at least — is strictly limited. Why? To some extent because people are reluctant to become involved in the largely unknown; but probably even more, because people still have a very restricted notion of the Church. They have not understood the extent of the Church's mission and therefore of the spheres where they can be apostolic — and in some cases already are being apostolic without realising that what they are doing is the work of the Church: that they are in fact *being* the Church in their daily lives. Some of this is due to the hang-over from the days when a specific mandate was required — almost before you could light the charcoal for the thurible for benediction. More vitally it is due to a very "clerical" approach to the Church, its works and pomps, by the laity themselves.

This is why I have gone to some length to explain the approach of the Second Vatican Council to the role of the layman — described by one journalist as emerging from the Council as a "kind of bowler-hatted monk":

the monk because presumably he is interested and involved in worship and the praise of God, and the bowler-hat presumably to reflect his commitment as a Christian in the world. It is not the happiest of phrases. I hope that the bowler-hat does not denote his enforced retirement from the scene from which in times gone by he was notably absent, if not excluded.

Even though there was this great release in the Council, we shall not find the answer to today's problems by taking our stand on the decree of 1965. Nor need we. There have been many developments since that time. But if we are going to learn from what has happened we should be looking at two points: first, has it been made possible for people to share in the life of the Church at local level? Second, have we so strangled ourselves with structure for structure's sake that we have forgotten the object of the exercise, the shedding of the light of the Gospel on the world in which we live?

"Through their baptism and confirmation *all* are commissioned to that apostolate by the Lord himself" we are told in the Constitution on the Church (art. 33). To be practical we know that we cannot even succeed in bringing all people to baptism. To be realistic we know that not all baptised Christians are willing to become involved in the direct work of the Church — though the number is probably higher than we imagine when we understand that such involvement for a layman lies primarily in his secular or non-churchy surroundings.

But willing or not, the obligation and responsibility are there. Means must be found to enable members of the ecclesial community (which we call the Church) to share in the life and mission to which they are called by Christ. There needs to be enough structure to ensure that the means are open to all and that the endeavour of Christian priests and laymen can be coordinated and directed for the effective fulfilment of the evangelising task given by the Lord to his people. People are often rude about "structure" nowadays. But without some structure, how in practice can we ensure for all the faithful (or more realistically, any of the faithful who are willing) the opportunity to enter into the apostolic life of the Church in their parish or in their diocese? Without some formalised set-up, the door is going to be closed or seem to be closed on the probably over-worked, frequently out-of-touch, one-man-band, or on the "in-group" drawn together on a personal basis.

Some kind of structures of dialogue are theologically necessary and administratively highly desirable. At all levels in the Church — internationally, nationally, in diocese, parish or small group — responsible decisions have to be taken in the cause of the Gospel. For these to be good decisions, those with the necessary knowledge and experience must be heard. They must share in the *making* of the decisions which someone (in virtue of his office) may ultimately have to *take*. But without some sort of structure of consultation (or dialogue) how can their voices be heard? How in fact can they fulfil their duty and responsibility? If you wonder if they really have that duty, let me quote again from the Council, this time from art. 37 of the Constitution on the Church:

> "Every layman should reveal to his sacred pastor his needs and desires with that freedom and confidence which befits a son of God and a brother in Christ. An individual layman, by reason of the knowledge, competence, or outstanding ability which he may enjoy, is permitted and sometimes even obliged to express his opinion on things which concern the good of the Church. When occasions arise, let this be done through the agencies set up by the Church for this purpose".

That is why I claim that certain basic structures are theologically necessary at every level in the Church. The necessity arises from the very nature of the Church. I believe that they are also administratively desirable. A weighty decision, taken without consulting others with varying experiences reflecting their different vocations and backgrounds, is under normal circumstances irresponsible and often wrong. Even if right, without consultation it is often unacceptable.

In practice, what has happened in the parishes, in the diocese, nationally and even internationally? Experiences will differ. But if I may generalise, the sad thing is that quite often long years have been given to the turgid task of preparing constitutions, orders of procedure, etc., which have sometimes ham-strung apostolic endeavour. Work has not always been halted. The work has gone on un-coordinated and not very effectively, and quite separate from a constitutionally valid parish or diocesan council which has driven apostles to despair and thrown great ideals into disrepute. An opposition grows against all meetings and even against all organisations and societies. In fact some coming together is highly valuable in a time where we have to learn from one another and exchange ideas and experiences. But all this is a means to the end which is spreading the Gospel, being "a living witness and a living instrument of the mission of the Church". That is also how we have to approach the role of a parish council.

Sadly consultation with the laity — at parish and diocesan level — is often thought to refer only to matters of finance and administration: almost as if these were the only spheres of non-clerical super-competence and interest. This is as wrong as it would be to tell a priest that he has no competence to express his interest and concern in anything outside his church-building: in, for example, an industrial dispute throwing half his parishioners out of work. In such a situation, priest and layman must consult and work together; and it is very much the same when it comes to deciding about the celebration of the parish feast or of the care of the old people in the area. Structures of dialogue must make sharing of responsibility possible, with the best possible use of the interest, experience and talents available. The structures should as far as possible reflect the make-up of the Church and then they will be concerned with the real work and mission of the Church, not just with a few inessential externals.

It may be that in some places opportunity is lacking. It is also important that even when we provide the opportunity we remember our responsibility to see that those invited to share have the formation or equipment they need. There is, of course, a chapter of the Decree on the Lay Apostolate dealing specifically with formation for the apostolate. It treats of spiritual formation, formation in the moral and social principles of the Church, formation in the means of giving one's witness to Christ most effectively at home and at work, and the whole study of how the work of formation is in itself continuous or, as we say, on-going throughout life, from primary catechesis to adult education. All this is in chapter VI of the decree.

The fundamental question remains. Is what we are doing really directed to the shedding of the light of the Gospel on the world in which we live?

On occasion I have been challenged as to the value of the time I must give to the Synod of Bishops, to the Council of which I was co-opted by Pope Paul. In all sincerity I have replied that, although the Synod is a very different body from an ecumenical council of the Church, nevertheless in some sense the Synod today developes the teaching of the Second Vatican Council. The 1974 Synod dealt with the subject of evangelisation and just twelve months later Pope Paul, following the advice offered, gave us that marvellous document on Evangelisation in the Modern World which we can recognise as a further instalment to the Council's Constitution on the Church.

For, having established the layman as a full and responsible member of the Church, we now go on to recognise that the Church is everywhere missionary and that to be baptised is to receive the call and responsibility to spread the Good News of the Gospel. In this he will be sharing in the life and work of Christ himself who said: "I must proclaim the Good News of the Kingdom of God" (Lk 4:43), and who told his disciples that they were to be his "witness to the ends of the earth" (Acts 1:8). Can we forget the words of St Paul: "Not that I boast of preaching the Gospel, since it is a duty that has been laid on me; I should be punished if I did not preach it" (1 Cor 9:16)?

In his letter on evangelisation Pope Paul calls our attention to words from the declaration issued from the 1974 Synod: "We wish to confirm once more that the task of evangelising all people constitutes the essential mission of the Church". He says that it is a task which the state of present-day society makes urgent but it has always been there. "The Church", he says, "is born of the evangelising activity of Jesus and the twelve". There is this profound link between Christ, the Church and evangelisation. It is a link which is not just for the institution but also for the individual member. The Gospel must be proclaimed explicitly and by the witness of personal life. The consequence of the layman *in* the Church is the important witness he must give in his own lay life and secular surroundings.

This letter on evangelisation stresses the importance of the ways and means of how to evangelise. Pope Paul emphasises that for the whole Church the first means must be "the witness of fidelity to the Lord Jesus — the witness of poverty and detachment, of freedom in the face of the powers of this world: in short, the witness of sanctity".

The verbal proclamation of Gospel truth is also indispensable, even though secondary today to that living witness to which the Pope has referred. He said that he is well aware that modern man is sated with talk, tired of listening and almost impervious to words. Thus it is necessary that we should have recourse to the modern means available for communication. By this I am not so much suggesting TV and Radio courses for clergy as understanding the use of Catholic laymen in these key areas of communications. We all complain at times about the power of the media. If the power is in the hands of those whose very lives reflect the way of the Gospel then there is a greater chance that it will be the image of Christ which underlies the message that comes into our homes. "The word becomes relevant when it is the bearer of the power of God" writes Pope Paul.

In exactly the same way we must recognise the importance of catechetical method as well as the personal example of the teacher. When it comes to sacramental living, we realise the emphasis placed today on the response required from the recipient of the grace of the sacrament. There has been a shift from mere membership of the Church and "sharing in salvific mission" to the basic idea that baptism means being an evangeliser. This is the task of the layman as well as the priest. Today lay apostolate means the work of evangelisation. This is not just playing with words. It is a most important development in our whole understanding of the layman in the Church.

"The whole Church is missionary and the work of evangelisation is a basic duty of the People of God". So Pope Paul reminds us with a quotation from the Second Vatican Council's Decree on the Church's Missionary Activity. There we are given the key to the question of the institutional Church and personal responsibility in the work of evangelisation, for the Pope says quite clearly that evangelisation is for no one an individual and isolated act; "it is one that is deeply ecclesial". The individual acts not in virtue of a mission which he attributes to himself or by a personal inspiration but in union with the mission of the Church and in her name. When we examine the structures we have established, we must ask ourselves whether they relate to the following words of the Pope: "If each individual evangelises in the name of the Church, no evangeliser is the absolute master of his evangelising action, with discretionary power to carry it out in accordance with individualistic criteria and perspectives; he acts in communion with the Church and her pastors".

This is why I claim that if all the baptised are to share Christ's work, there must be certain basic structures so that they may relate to one another and ensure a fair degree of co-ordination of activity. The value of Christ's work demands this. It must also be remembered that in relation to a universal Church, the word "ecclesial" has a world-wide connotation. This applies both to missionary responsibility and in some way to the structures by which the efforts of the faithful are related. The very structure of the Church helps our understanding of this because we see that differing ministries and vocations determine the different spheres where we evangelise and they underlie the relationship between us and our work.

There is little point in my trying to improve on Pope Paul's words:

> "Lay people, whose particular vocation places them in the midst of the world and in charge of the most varied temporal tasks, must for this very reason exercise a very special form of evangelisation.
>
> "Their primary and immediate task is not to establish and develop the ecclesial community — this is the specific role of the pastors — but to put to use every Christian and evangelical possibility latent but already present and active in the affairs of the world. Their own field of evangelising activity is the vast and complicated world of politics, society and economics, but also the world of culture, of the sciences and the arts, of international life, of the mass media. It also includes realities which are open to evangelisation, such as human love, the family, the education of children and adolescents, professional work, suffering. The more Gospel-inspired lay people there are engaged in these realities, clearly involved in them, competent to promote them and conscious that they must exercise to the full their Christian powers which are often buried and suffocated, the more these realities will be at the service of the Kingdom of God and therefore of salvation in Jesus Christ".

For myself I am happy to see "lay auxiliaries to the hierarchy" and even "lay apostles" give way to the phrase

"Gospel-inspired lay people". That surely must be the present ideal in a steadily advancing process. And amidst so much development and change what is to be preserved? I give the last word suitably enough to the Vicar of Christ, whose image we seek to project:

> "Let us therefore preserve our fervour of spirit. Let us preserve the delightful and comforting joy of evangelising, even when it is in tears that we must sow. May it mean for us — as it did for John the Baptist, for Peter and Paul, for the other apostles and for a multitude of splendid evangelisers all through the Church's history — an interior enthusiasm that nobody and nothing can quench. May it be the great joy of our consecrated lives. And may the world of our time, which is searching, sometimes with anguish, sometimes with hope, be enabled to receive the Good News not from evangelisers who are dejected, but from ministers of the Gospel whose lives glow with fervour, who have first received the joy of Christ, and who are willing to risk their lives so that the Kingdom may be proclaimed and the Church established in the midst of the world".

FORMATION AT THE GRASS-ROOTS

The importance of formation is generally recognised by those who are active in the mission of the Church. It seems unlikely that there can be grounds for serious disagreement on the theory of formation. On the other hand there is an increasing volume of experience about ways in which this same theory is to be put into practice. If then the approach is to be practical, it is unlikely that there is a blue-print for universal application. We have constantly to be asking ourselves: Formation for what? We may answer in general terms: "To give witness to Christ and to share in the salvific mission of the Church". But it is clear that the manner in which this is to be done will vary in accord with local circumstances and needs.

It is important, therefore, that we should be adaptable in putting the theory of formation into practice. The emphasis of Conciliar teaching is on the consequences of baptism and the responsibilities of all the baptised to share in the life and apostolate of the Church. Therefore, whatever realistic limitations may be set by our experience, we have to claim that the apostolate is for all and that therefore, at least in theory, apostolic formation must be available to all. Herein lies the problem. Even if we say it must be personal, though not individual, it must still be "at base". That is why we speak of formation at the grass-roots. One could go further and say that many of the troubles and frustrations experienced by the Church in her attempts to renew herself have arisen from attempts to hand out (or seize) new responsibilities in the life of the Church without adequate formation or even information.

Formation is directed to this life as well as to the next. Our witness to Christ is here as well as hereafter. We are not to regard formation as spiritual equipment to enable us to do battle in the world as if it were enemy territory. Our task is to focus the whole world upon Christ and this means living Christianity in the world today. Our formation will therefore develop not merely by study but by doing. You cannot become proficient at golf merely by reading about it. First you look through the manual and then you get out on the golf-course and start hitting the ball. It is the same with our Christian life. We need to study the rules but then get out into the world (i.e. our local community) and try to put them into effect. The process is continuous. Experience reveals new problems, all of which have to be studied. But if we do not keep on practising, our Christian life becomes academic, speculative, unrealistic and sometimes an anachronism.

There can be no doubt of the principle of "needs before structure". The layman will discover his field of apostolate as soon as he seeks out and tries to meet the needs of his neighbour. On the other hand, though we may be unprofessional in our first efforts, we soon see the need to try to perfect our methods if we are to do justice to Christian truth and practice. We have to determine the best way of acting in our own particular circumstances. This may mean asking others, discussion, study, and most certainly prayer. In all this we have somehow to preserve the delicate balance between the theoretical and the practical. Lectures themselves are not enough. Neither is the haphazard method of trial by error. But the point is really this. When a man is brought to see the facts and is able to evaluate the needs of those about him, then he will want to improve the manner of the service he must give in the name of Christ.

Who is to initiate the efforts of the searching layman? Whence does he receive the call to action, to share in the life and work of the Church? How is he to perfect the manner of his apostolic action? Very frequently the call will come from the priest, ordained to proclaim the word of God and administer the sacraments. The manner in which that call is made will vary. The call itself may be indirect: delivered to one layman by another who has heard it. But the task of calling laymen to the apostolate and of helping in their formation must be seen as a part of the normal role of a priest, not something exceptional. Indeed it is an extension of his sacral role, the furtherance of his work of baptising and administering the Eucharist. To say this is neither paternalism nor clericalism. It is for the priest to call and sustain. But whilst his task in this may be indispensable, the formation given to laymen must be such as to enable them also to carry out their indispensable role in the Church.

If we admit that specialised formation for specialised apostolates will be given in special circumstances, e.g. at centres of formation or to a selected number of members of an association of committed Christians, what principles of basic formation are we left with? In general, formation must be spiritual, doctrinal (to include the social teaching of the Church), professional or technical, suited to the needs of the times and of the person, and given in practice as well as taught in theory.

There must be spiritual formation. Article 4 of the decree reminds us that the success of the apostolate "depends on the layman's oneness with Christ. This oneness with Christ, nourished by the life of the Church, especially by the liturgy, must not be considered separate from the ordinary duties of daily life". The spirituality of the layman must be something personal, and spiritual formation must be relevant to his needs and circumstances. But it must also be related to his membership of the Christian community, and it must be developed to enable him both to play his part in the liturgical worship of the

Church and to meet the needs of others. However, emphasis on the communal nature of worship must not be at the expense of his personal relationship as an individual creature with his God and redeemer. Indeed private prayer will assist him to prepare for his role in family and community prayer. But it would be wrong to restrict a consideration of spirituality to the notion of prayer. It will be expressed in many ways, not least his loving service of his fellow-men.

Formation in the spiritual life is likely to take many forms and will acquire new aspects in relation to the changing needs both of the individual and of the community. "The spiritual life of lay people must be adapted to their circumstances, depending on their age and state of health, their work and social surroundings, and whether they are single, married or widowed. Each situation has its own blessings which must be developed, along with one's personal God-given talents".

Formation is often a mutual process. People help to form one another. Clearly the priest has a special responsibility not only to give spiritual formation but to strive to understand the condition and needs of the persons he has to form. He will be greatly helped by the measure in which the lay people make known their needs to him and give him insight into their problems by making him aware of the true nature of any of their circumstances which he may be unable to share with them. But before all else this oneness with Christ, which is the ideal of spiritual formation, will be achieved through a profound sacramental life. Here again we see the importance of the priest's role, both as administrator of the sacraments and as counsellor, confidant and friend.

There must be doctrinal formation. Clearly the layman must have a good knowledge of the teaching of Christ and of his Church. The gospels are not to be regarded as academic literature or even as a book of rules. They are essentially a way of life in which the Christian must be formed if he himself is to proclaim God's word by speech and by example. For this reason the formation given must be suited to his capacity but also relevant to his needs and the problems he actually experiences in this life. The Gospel teaching must be seen in the light of his own circumstances and he must be shown how the tenets of the Church have a bearing on his own conduct. The layman's faith must be lively but it will grow in proportion to his understanding. He cannot exercise his co-responsibility in the work of the Church without the means of increasing his knowledge of its doctrine. This applies to teaching concerning the life to come as well as to the manner of Christian conduct in this life.

Pope John XXIII stressed the importance of this in his encyclical *Mater et Magistra*: "Since the education of Christians is concerned with duties in every department of life, the teaching they receive must inspire the faithful to make their conduct conform to the Church's teaching in economic and social matters . . . It is not enough to tell them in what manner the Church teaches that Christians ought to act in social and economic affairs. Of equal importance is it that ways be indicated to them by which they may effectively carry out their duties . . . It has almost become a proverb that no one can learn the right use of freedom except by using freedom rightly. So also, no one learns how properly to observe Catholic teaching in social and economic affairs except by putting social principles into action".

This doctrinal formation has to be related to the age and capacity of the person. Clearly in this matter, as in all other aspects of formation, it must be progressive. It begins in the home, is developed in school and often finds practical expression as the layman reaches maturity. But it is never concluded. Throughout life the apostolic layman, like the priest, has to continue to plumb the profound depths of the treasury of the Christian religion, as he seeks after the perfection which is his goal. There may be examination certificates and diplomas to be won in certain departments of social science but no human can ever acquit

105

himself of the responsibility to try to learn more of the truths of an infinite God.

There must be professional formation. Holy simplicity and humility may be virtues. Inefficiency and hanging back from giving Christian witness are not. Our talents are from God and we owe it to God to carry out the work entrusted to us in the most effective way. The layman's task lies especially in secular matters, and therefore he has the responsibility not only to present Christian truth in the best possible light but also to penetrate his secular surroundings to the greatest extent and with the best possible use of his talents. The sphere of his influence for good will increase in proportion with his being good at his job. This does not mean that he necessarily has to strive to achieve the highest position in his profession, but it does mean that no one is likely to heed his Christian witness if he is no good at his professional job.

Every man has the right and duty to develop his natural potentialities. This must be taken into consideration in the formation given to the layman. In fairly primitive conditions it may even happen that the priest himself will have to initiate the giving of such professional formation, though this is less likely today than it was in the past. But certainly he has to struggle with his people to ensure that such professional or technical formation is available to them. There is a danger of paternalism here but some-one has to take the initiative. Gradually those formed will assume their proper responsibility. Professional formation is a continuous process, not merely because of the steady need for personal development but because the needs which the layman must meet in the name of Christ are constantly changing. Often the work of the priest will be to bring his people to see the necessity of their overcoming the frequently-heard objection: "It is no use my trying to do anything. I lack professional competence (or, I do not know how)".

Of course one must not overlook the question of personal ability. As a rider to this principle, it is evident that persons unable to tackle a particular problem for lack of natural competence or even lack of opportunity should try to ensure that such means of formation are available to others better suited for the task.

Formation must be relevant. Whenever one considers the work of formation, from whatever aspect and whatever level, one comes back to the fact that it must be suited to the needs of the persons concerned. In this sense it has to be contemporary. We may talk nonsense when we speak of "new spirituality" because the relationship between God and one of his creatures does not change. But the circumstances in which that relationship is given expression change and these are factors which have to be borne in mind even in liturgical worship, e.g. the whole idea of active participation in the Church's worship bears a close relation to the aspiration of men today to share actively in government and in the education they receive. Thus we see that formation today can never be imposed. It is something which must be worked out between both the "former" and the person to be "formed". Indeed the process is of mutual benefit. No one is beyond further formation.

Methods of formation must take into consideration not only the capacity of the individual but also temperament, national characteristics, age, sex, and local needs and problems. This applies equally to the circumstances in which the formation is to be given. But if in large measure formation is being carried out in practice, then almost inevitably it will be related to the needs and capacity of the persons concerned. There is no doubt that theoretical training may easily be unrealistic and this is particularly true when it is being given to a group of persons of identical background, of limited experience and interest. The mission of like to like is a well-known adage. The formation of like by like has certain obvious limitations. But if formation is to be apt, there must be understanding of needs and characteristics.

Formation must be given in practice. This aspect of

formation has already been emphasised. But further stress should be laid on the desirability of its being carried out in a communal context. Many of the problems in life today arise because men live alongside one another, though not together. It is in this setting that the layman must be formed for his apostolate. The Christian spirit is a communal spirit. As Joseph Cardijn wrote: "One cannot bear witness alone, just as one cannot be saved alone. It is essential to discover each other as brothers on a completely equal footing. If the priest is the animator and the educator, this is all the more reason for him to remember that laymen form themselves amongst themselves through brotherly contact with one another and an inter-action which permits all individual qualities and responsibilities to be brought into play. Common commitment is common responsibility for the solutions adopted for the problems of life" (*Laymen into action*). We see therefore that if formation is to be given in practice, it cannot be given in isolation.

Formation is best given in small groups. And so at last we come to the heart of the matter, especially where the grass-roots are concerned. Both because it is impractical to give this formation individually and because it is desirable that laymen are formed in a communal setting, formation is best given to small groups. The numbers making up a group may vary according to age but generally groups should consist of about twelve to twenty persons. Groups larger than this seldom permit personal involvement which is necessary before there can be communal commitment. If possible these groups should reflect the local community and therefore desirably they should normally include men and women, drawn from varying professional experience.

Because the laymen are to be formed for an apostolate in secular spheres, the groups should meet under secular conditions and in secular surroundings such as the homes of their members. It may mean that the numbers involved in this type of formation are initially small but, once formed, they will be able to assist in the formation of others. There is no short cut to this, and if it takes place within the structure of a parish, it is clearly desirable that a priest be present to assist in the work of formation. But it must be realised that the process is not confined to such meetings. It continues in action between the gatherings at which experience gained can be exchanged. This type of formation cannot be haphazard and the meetings of the groups must be prepared. One of the principal problems, especially in the early days, will be the provision of programme material and here Catholic organisations must cooperate in the preparation of general guidelines. Care must be taken lest this be too stereotyped, thereby depriving the formation of its essential realism and relevance.

Always the problem is how to start. Often people can be brought together on an area or neighbourhood basis, possibly assembled in the first place to meet and discuss some local problems. To invite people to group themselves together without some real and already experienced bond or interest seldom produces a widespread response. This is not due to lack of goodwill or even to the desire not to become involved. It is usually a failure of the individual to appreciate his responsibility or to realise that he is capable of making any contribution of value. This will not be overcome without at least a partial understanding of the nature and membership of the Church. It is this realisation, before all else, that priests must strive to bring to the laity.

"Pastors know that they themselves were not meant by Christ to shoulder alone the entire saving mission of the Church toward the world. On the contrary they understand that it is their noble duty so to shepherd the faithful and recognise their services and charismatic gifts that all according to their proper roles may cooperate in this common undertaking with one heart" (*Lumen Gentium,* 30).

HOW A PARISH COUNCIL WORKS

If we accept that all Christians are called to the apostolate, and take a broad view of the Church and of its mission, it is clear that for the efforts of all concerned to be effective, there must be some sort of co-ordination and even direction. At various levels responsible decisions must be made. For these to be good decisions, those with the necessary knowledge and experience must be heard. Without some sort of structure of consultation (or dialogue) how can their voices be heard? How can they fulfil their baptismal responsibility?

Again, the Second Vatican Council (in the Constitution on the Church) has something to say about this: "An individual layman by reason of the knowledge, competence, or outstanding ability which he may enjoy, is permitted and sometimes even obliged to express his opinion on things which concern the good of the Church. When occasions arise, let this be done through the agencies set up by the Church for this purpose" (*Lumen Gentium,* 37).

In claiming, therefore, that there is good theological backing for a parish council, we are not losing sight of the fact that it is also highly desirable from point of view of parish administration. Clearly if a large number of people are to be engaged in the work of Christ there must be some coordination of their efforts to make them effective. Otherwise you have muddle and overlapping, and possibly whole areas which are neglected. What is more, through a council it is possible for the expert knowledge of an individual to be placed at the disposal of the parish and to some extent shared with the other parishioners.

Why do you need a parish council to coordinate the work? It is often said that the priest already knows who are the real workers and who is the best person for each job. Let him ask when he wants help: he does not need a council for that. Such a claim is based on a very limited picture of the Church, its works and the responsibilities of its members. It is probably true if we are thinking only of first communion breakfasts, arranging summer fêtes and even organising planned giving. But is this an adequate picture of the Church's work and interest?

Think of the extent of the mission given to the parishioners: to take Christ's truths to all men. You realise then that it includes liturgical worship, the care of the sick and elderly and those in need, provision for young people and the catechetical instruction of children, not to mention adult education. Then there is work for Christian unity, the evangelisation of non-believers, social welfare, civic life, the whole field of industry and the missionary activity of the Church — all this in addition to parish administration and finance. Even if the priest is a wizard and knows the best men and women for all these jobs, the right hand should know what the left is doing. There must be some means of exchange of information. In practice, the exchange of ideas will also make much of the work more effective.

With the proper notion of the size of the job, the number of active persons required becomes obvious. No one can pretend that the priest can cope with all this, even if he wishes — not if the work is to be undertaken on the scale needed. Even more important is the realisation that all parishioners have a duty and right to share in this work. It is not the special work of an "in-group". Again we see that without some organisation, the work cannot be tackled adequately, nor can parishioners share in the various decisions and initiatives.

We can see this in respect of the parish itself and also in the wider community we are called to serve with our fellow-Christians. The opportunities are so many that there must be some order about it. Though all the people in the parish share responsibility for this work, inevitably and rightly the task of leading and inspiring lies with the priest. In his work of coordination he will need the help and cooperation of his people. Even from this point of view of administration, there is a case for a council at which he will either preside or be the chairman.

The Decree on the Lay Apostolate set a wide target for parish councils — and for others to be set up at diocesan and national levels. "Through the cooperation of clergy and religious with lay people, such councils can assist the apostolic work of the Church both in evangelising and sanctifying, and in charitable, social and other endeavours. They will be helpful for the mutual coordination of various lay enterprises and organisations without threatening the autonomy and special character of each group" (*Apostolicam Actuositatem,* 26).

There is no blueprint for all parish councils. Local needs vary and so must the organisation set up to deal with them. There is therefore no uniform constitution for all parishes, laying down what a council must do and how it must do it. Such statements of purpose as exist are usually not so much definitions of objectives as descriptions of how a group of parishioners act together.

Some constitutions are rather obviously theology-conscious, describing the role of the parish and even of the Church rather than the task of a parish council. As a general introduction to shared responsibility this is no bad thing, but they give you the spirit rather than the letter of the law. Here are three samples:

1. "The purpose of the parish council is to enable parishioners to participate more fully in the life of the

113

Church, as expressed in the decrees of the Second Vatican Council".

2. "The council's task is to coordinate as well as initiate and promote the various facets of the mission of the Church — to make known the mission of Christ and to restore all things in him".

3. "The purpose of the parish council is to enable priests and people to make Christ present in our midst as God's people on pilgrimage through a largely indifferent world. The council should therefore discuss and plan the whole life, work and worship of the parish: the whole field of man as a member of the Church and a citizen of the world".

To offset these theologically orientated paragraphs, it is not unusual to find a more pragmatic statement of intent which says simply: "The parish council is to advise the parish priest in all aspects of development in the parish" — or even "To advise the parish priest in all matters where he seeks advice". This may help to reassure those anxious lest the establishment of a parish council is a take-over bid in disguise, but if it is all that is said, it is scarcely adequate.

In his valuable booklet, *Catholic Parish Council Handbook,* Bernard Bligh attempts a model constitution in which he sets out the purpose of the council as follows:

a. "To advise the parish priest on any point on which he seeks advice.

b. "To survey regularly any needs referred to it by the parish priest and to advise him on satisfying the needs.

c. "To survey regularly any resources referred to it by the parish priest and to advise him on making full use of the resources.

d. "To undertake any work assigned to the council by the parish priest with its agreement".

This may be a good practical way of making a beginning or even of clarifying the consultative role of the council but in the end something more clearly reflecting the nature and mission of the Church will be desirable. For though it is true that in the Church there are different ministries, vocations and responsibilities, "yet all share a true equality with regard to the dignity and to the activity common to all the faithful for the building up of the Body of Christ" (*Lumen Gentium*, 32). The search for a clear definition of functions of a parish council should avoid the danger of legalising paternalism.

In many ways, provided that there is a good understanding of relationships between those at first concerned, it will often be better not to attempt a formal constitution with precise statement of purpose and manner of operation until the provisional council has had perhaps a year's experience of working together. Then theological nicety can be balanced with practical experience. It will be sad if a parish council cannot have both. Members should work out their own formula and not take the easy way of adopting en bloc another council's constitution. In certain aspects it may not fit. Needs will determine the purpose as well as the best way of working. It takes time to be sure about needs.

Parish councils have a consultative role. Often the word "only" is added. This suggests inadequacy and restriction. Is it worthwhile to give time to the work of a parish council unless it has what people call "a real say" in things? This is a common enough question but it is based on a misunderstanding.

The misunderstanding arises from the difficulty of trying to ensure the sharing of responsibility in a hierarchical structure, i.e. in a body where there is order based on the authority and responsibility related to office and ministry. The truth is that whilst each individual Christian is "permitted and sometimes even obliged to express his opinion on things which concern the good of the Church" (*Lumen Gentium*, 37), there are also certain individuals who, because of the office they hold, have the sole right and duty to take whatever decision is necessary.

The classic example lies with the Pope, who shares certain responsibilities with the other bishops throughout the world and who hears what they have to say before as Pope he takes the decision and makes formal pronouncement. The bishops share with him the burden involved in collecting all the views and experiences he needs to make a responsible decision. But he takes the decision. In the same way the bishop hears his canons or council of priests (and ideally his diocesan pastoral council) before taking the important decision which is his by virtue of the burden of office he bears. They share in the making of the decision he takes. Their role, though immensely important, is consultative.

This distinction between decision-taking and decision-making is essential to our understanding of the consultative role of most of the structures recommended by the Second Vatican Council. It reflects the whole make-up of the Church. When people say that a consultative role is pointless, and that consultative bodies "have no teeth" they have not really begun to understand co-responsibility in a hierarchical Church.

The full force of this is seen when we realise the nature of a parish council's responsibilities and the kind of matter it is dealing with. Its scope is as wide as the Church itself. Clearly if the parish council is trying to decide at what time the Lord Mayor will open the summer fête, it will not normally be necessary for the parish priest to take the decision which they have shared in making. But if the bishop asks the priests to discover the views of parish councils regarding a matter such as "communion in the hand", then it is not for the parish council to decide how the parishioners will receive Holy Communion the following Sunday. Their views are passed on to the bishop so that he may know the mind of his people when he has to vote on the issue at a meeting of the Bishops' Conference.

In fact relatively few of the matters dealt with by a parish council call for a decision by vote. If the members are considering the social needs of people in the district or how to help their fellow-parishioners to a greater knowledge of the Scriptures or the Church's moral teaching, these are matters of strategy when a good working arrangement must be worked out together. Sometimes there may be different opinions with regard, for example, to the percentage of parish income to be given each year to the missions. But the decision will not really rest with the parish priest who would be most unwise and most unlikely to set aside the advice he is given by his people.

What is the priest's role in this? He is the leader of the parish where he represents the bishop, to whom primarily he is responsible and from whom he draws his authority. For all the emphasis there is today on the idea of co-responsibility and sharing by the people of God, there is no point in pretending that the Church is a participatory democracy, with authority drawn from the people.

Certainly, in many things the priest is before God answerable to the people he serves. But his power to take certain decisions is drawn from the bishop of the diocese where he serves. Therefore, whether we call his office that of president of the parish council or chairman, he is the leader of the council which he consults in certain important decisions he must take and whose members are his fellow-workers in the task of spreading the Gospel in his parish. He must call them to this special role in the apostolate and train them for their task.

The temptation to supply a blueprint for general use in setting up a parish council is to be resisted as firmly as surrendering to the request for a uniform constitution for adoption in every parish. The first concern must be the examination of local needs: not just the local brand of social problem but what the parish needs to enable it to fulfil its proper mission. Only when this is clear can one begin to see the organisation needed in the parish to meet the situation.

Certain basic requirements are almost bound to turn up in every parish, e.g., how the whole parish is to take an effective part in the liturgy. But numbers of members and frequency of meetings, etc., must depend upon the kind of work to be undertaken and the kind of organisation which is needed. If, on the other hand, a parish starts merely by importing someone else's constitution and following precisely the same pattern of getting to work, the chances are that it will stagnate and die of inanition even before it has found itself.

A parish council comes into existence in stages. There is no other way of making sure that it fits the local situation or that the people concerned are convinced that it is needed precisely because they have tried to think about what is required. The best way of beginning is for the parish priest to call together half a dozen or more of his trusted helpers with varied experience and whose opinion he and his parishioners respect. Obviously there is a danger here that the leading members of the "old guard" may meet together, don new hats and ensure no more than the continuation of the status quo. On the other hand, if the priest calls in six parishioners who have played no active part in parish affairs in the past, it is unlikely that they will be in a position to make an accurate assessment. Their conclusions will seldom command support from those in the "know" or even from the priest.

So the sensible thing is for the priest to gather together a few of his special helpers and add to their number one or two others who have experience of this kind of work, e.g., in local government or the social services, etc. It is no bad thing to include a couple of young people, though their help and presence in the eventual council will be of greater value than in this original working-party. If the parish is wide-spread or there is one section especially associated with a chapel-of-ease in the parish, it will be important to have a member drawn from that area.

Above all the priest himself must be associated with the working-party from the very beginning. If he hides his mistrust of the whole idea by saying that he is handing over to the laity and they must have a free hand in making their recommendations, he is undermining the entire operation and, incidentally, presenting a false picture of the Church. Unless priest and parishioner work together, whatever is eventually set up is more likely to impede the apostolate than to promote it.

What is the working-party to do? The first thing is to find out what is being done in the parish in the name of the Church. There may be groups and lay organisations trying to deepen their own spirituality and to carry out certain charitable works. There may be a group of "collectors" and men who help the priest in the unenviable but inevitable task of raising money. There will probably be an altar servers' guild and there may be a choir and a youth club. But what about the other needs and about those parts of the parishioners' lives which are not often thought of as having any direct connection with religion, such as local unemployment or the lack of nursery school facilities for the children of mothers having to go out to work? Is there perhaps a new estate in the parish where those who have just arrived in the area feel fish out of water?

Often when such a working party meets together for the first time it is suggested that there are no needs not already met or known. As a tentative list is drawn up and becomes longer, then there is a switch round and the task seems almost too formidable to be practical. Why should not the local community services cope? There is no special responsibility for the Church. Are we playing our part in that community? Would we just be duplicating effort by setting up our own organisation . . .? Experience shows that the initial sense of pointlessness soon gives way to doubts as to whether the parish can possibly cope with all there is to be done.

When the list of needs is set against known resources, thought should be given to establishing groups to try to tackle specific tasks or spheres of responsibility: in some cases an existing organisation can take on a particular job or area of concern. It may be necessary to have half a dozen or more such groups. When the general headings have been decided and the problems located, then a parish meeting should be called and people chosen to serve on one of these groups or given the task of recruiting helpers. We can imagine groups for liturgy, ecumenism, education or catechetics, youth, social welfare, missionary activity, finance and social activities. There could well be others.

Once these groups are set up, there is the basis for representation to a parish council. Let each group choose one or two representatives. Where there are distinct districts in a parish it is useful if a local spokesman is chosen. Ideally these members should be elected by those they represent. Sometimes this is not possible for at least a year because people do not know each other well enough to elect. The passage of time and proven abilities help to resolve this difficulty. Where there is this local ignorance of other Catholics, it can be useful to arrange house Masses in an area, and following discussion after the Mass, a choice can be made.

There will always be need for certain ex-officio members who may not otherwise be known or thought of in the more secular side of parish life. This can include people like the head teacher of the parish primary school, or the principal altar-server or M.C. Equally there may be a Catholic on the local council with little time for other parish work: it can be useful to make provision for a limited number of co-options. Care should be taken to see that there are two young people chosen by their peers.

From all these groupings in the parish and including established lay organisations, representation can be achieved which can form the parish council. Let them have a provisional existence of at least one year and only then should they try to work out a simple constitution based on their experience of working together. Even that should be subject to review twelve months later.

If the parish council consists largely of members representing groups who are getting on with one or other aspect of the work of the Church, then the role of the council will to some extent be that of coordination. But there will always be a certain number of things which can only be undertaken by the council as such. The meetings must be sufficiently frequent to keep all the members in touch with what is going on or is planned, and to ensure an adequate exchange of advice and experience when it is wanted, not as a post mortem two months afterwards.

Again, one is reluctant to lay down a precise time-table but experience suggests that, at least in the early stages of a parish council's existence, it should meet monthly. Otherwise no matters of real importance, requiring timely advice, will ever be referred to it. It will be more like an annual meeting to receive reports of what has been done rather than a pooling of ideas and energies about what should be done. Monthly meetings will also ensure a reasonably short agenda and meetings which are not too long.

It goes without saying that an efficient secretary is needed and that there should be a prepared agenda and reasonably detailed minutes. It is always important to remember that each group or its representative does not have to report on all its activities at every meeting. Indeed the monthly meeting should not be confused with the council itself. Most of a good council's work is done between meetings but to implement decisions and policy made at meetings. But the other parishioners need to know what is happening.

Is the parish council just a sounding board, or a means for improved communications in the parish? The councillors are essentially the close collaborators of the parish priest in the work of the Gospel. Their job is to share in the work of spreading the Gospel and encouraging others to live a Christian life. Their meetings should reflect this. They are not a debating society or a prayer group. Their meetings are a means to apostolic action and are not

I

themselves the object of the exercise, even though they may help in the formation of those present.

So when we speak about how a parish council works we are not just describing the mechanics of its monthly meetings. Its members will be available for consultation but most of them will be actively engaged in the apostolate in the parish. As councillors they will often be leading groups of parishioners who share in the local mission of the Church. Some examples of what is meant may help.

It is quite possible that in addition to the priest there will be a lay representative from the parish working in the local Christian Council or Council of Churches. It will be for him to bring ideas and new developments to his parish but he will also have to be active contributing the views of the Church to local ecumenical initiatives. Where active help is wanted for some project such as a housing scheme, it will be for him to report to his parish council and there arrange ways in which such help may be forthcoming from the parish.

There may be some "Friday groups" in the parish, arranging weekly donations to developing countries from savings made through personal sacrifices. It could be useful if there is on the council a member to coordinate and promote the establishment of such groups; he should act as the parish link with CAFOD and make sure that the rest of the parish know what is happening. If there is to be some sponsored money-raising effort, through the council he can seek the help of others, especially the young people. The priest, seeing such generosity and good will, can arrange a special Mass for the groups and make reference to their work in his Sunday homily.

Nowadays many parishes have a liturgy group who work with their priest in helping him to meet the needs of his people and in providing the response he wants to the liturgy at which he presides. The group will probably include the M.C. and the choir-leader. One of the group may well be responsible for arranging the rota of readers at Mass and for seeing they are there when they are wanted. The group will also be able to help with the Bidding Prayers and the choice of those taking part in the offertory procession. It can be useful if the leader of the group, representing it on the parish council — or else the parish council secretary — read out whatever notices are needed at the end of the Mass, though ideally these are covered in a parish newsletter.

Bidding Prayers are a good example of what can and should be done. They are the prayers of the people and should be petitions representing the needs and intentions of the parish community. No printed book of Bidding Prayers can meet every occasion or suit every place. Ideally at least each parish should produce its own prayers each Sunday. This may sound a great deal of extra trouble. Yet it is possible, practical and is clearly right. It may be that the priest knows his people so well and can anticipate their needs so precisely that he can interpret their wishes and write the petitions himself. But they are the prayers of the *people*. The priest's task is to introduce the intentions and afterwards to commend them to God.

Here surely is a job for the parish council — or for a liturgy group with a representative on the council. Such a person should gather the intentions each week and then either write the petitions or hand them in to the presbytery to be written. A trivial example? No, a small instance of the sort of thing that happens when a parish comes alive on discovering how it can exercise its responsibilities in the life, mission and worship of the Church.

Lest all these examples of parish council activity may sound very inward-looking or "churchy", we should not forget such matters as social welfare and even finance and administration. Most parishes have their groups of collectors and fund-raisers. Clearly these must continue their work and be adequately represented on the parish council. The same goes for any social committee, whether its purpose is developing the parish community or raising money for parish needs. But in most parishes there are nowadays individuals or groups or lay organisations engaged in the relief of material need. Here again there is almost continuous work, such as the care of the sick and visiting the elderly and housebound. Those engaged in this kind of work should have a representative on the council, through which activities can be properly directed and, if necessary, help obtained.

Nor can we forget the work of the larger community of which the parish is part. "The apostolate of the social milieu, that is, the effort to infuse a Christian spirit into the mentality, customs, laws and structures of the community in which a person lives, is so much the duty and responsibility of the laity that it can never be properly performed by others. In this area the laity can exercise the apostolate of like to like. It is here that laymen add to the testimony of life the testimony of their speech; it is here in the arena of their labour, profession, studies, residence, leisure, and companionship that laymen have a special opportunity to help their brothers" (*Apostolicam Actuositatem*, 13). This section from the Decree on the Lay Apostolate should be constantly before the parish council.

The development of the parish as a community, with a parish council to help give it direction, is an important means of drawing as many as possible into the mission Christ gave to his Church. Parochialism is a major obstacle to such development. If the parish develops an "us and them" mentality and thinks only of its sufficiency or well-being, it ceases to be an instrument of evangelisation. A parish council, once it gets over the early temptation to be merely a supervisory or administrative body, is an excellent means of extending the work and vision of the local Church.

Once a parish begins to realise its potential, it sees its role in the wider Church. The parish council grows to appreciate that however close the bond of the parish community, the parish is in many things too small a unit for effective apostolic action. Education is a good example of this. The parents in a parish may want to work for a primary school or to play their part in a secondary school with a large catchment area. It is essential that they work together with the parents of adjoining parishes. Still better, through a close relationship between the parish councils of the area, the representatives of the parishes can consult together, coordinate the whole presentation of their case to the local authority and work together to achieve what may be needed.

Not in education alone. The situation may vary between urban parishes in one large town and scattered parishes in rural territory but both in communication and joint action the work of parish councils is often happily brought together in deanery pastoral councils. On these all the parishes of the deanery are represented, with meetings perhaps quarterly. But again the meeting is not the whole work of the council and through groups and committees the continuing work of the Church in the area of the deanery constantly goes ahead.

To relate the work of the deaneries, there is the diocesan pastoral council ... and so we lay ourselves open to the charge of structure-building almost for the sake of it. Needs will determine the structure but, most important of all, through groups and organisations and councils of this kind the individual Catholic layman begins to find his place in the apostolate of the Church.

CHRISTIANS IN THE WORLD

During the Second Vatican Council I was amongst those given the task of preparing a document on the Church in the World Today. It took a great deal of time because so many questions were involved. The journalists used to say that we were trying to cover everything "from the pill to the bomb". That would have been difficult enough, but really we were trying to write about a mystery. How was it that God, the maker of all things, seemed in large measure to have been rejected by the world? Why were the teachings of Christ's Church regarded by many as utterly irrelevant to their way of living and to their real problems?

One of the main difficulties was the fact that most Christians regard the world as enemy territory which has somehow to be conquered by other-worldly forces. True, we can make real distinctions between heaven and earth. But we have to remember that Christ's Church is incarnate in the world, that he founded it as the means by which all creation should be restored to the Father. It is when we forget this that we feel overwhelmed.

We should not have been surprised some years ago when we heard the words of Genesis read to the earth by the astronauts encircling the moon. But we were. So great is the apparent gap between so-called modern science and our centuries-old religion that we were almost more astonished that such men should proclaim the word of God than that we should be able to hear them at all. Equally we are sadly apt to marvel when people in certain walks of life preserve the integrity of their public and private existence amidst so many contaminating influences. Perhaps we think too much of the Church *and* the world, rather than the Church *in* the world.

Of course, we do not pretend that everything in the garden is lovely. Nor was it in the Garden of Eden — after man had separated himself from God's love. In the world today we see all manner of contradictions. Extravagance and poverty exist side by side. Scientific discovery in the service of mankind frequently serves merely to underline the unequal distribution of the world's goods. Generous love of the under-privileged often expresses itself in hatred and violence. The increase in personal freedom has led to a lack of restraint which can be a danger to public morality. But the greatest sign of contradiction is the failure to understand that these things are the concern of our Christian religion and way of life.

Often we Christians are deterred from entering fully into the life of the world in which Christ has set his Church by the very number and complexity of the problems which face us. We feel inadequate and out of our depth. So we make this neat separation of religion from life. We try not to get too much involved in one or the other. We forget that religion *is* our way of life, wherever we are, from one end of the day to the other. To feel inadequate is no bad thing if only it will inspire us to prepare ourselves for the task to be done. To feel out of our depth in this world merely underlines the truth that we are destined for a heavenly kingdom.

The Fathers of the Second Vatican Council recognised the danger that Catholics might become so engrossed in giving the Church a new look that they might lose sight of their essential mission to evangelise the world, to focus it on the teaching of the gospel. So, in the Constitution on The Church in the World Today, they pointed to some (not all) of the key areas where Christian witness is required: marriage and the family; the social and economic order; the whole field of modern culture and its relation to faith; political life; and peace and the world community. It was an immense programme. "Let us take pains", they wrote, "to pattern ourselves after the Gospel, more exactly every day, and thus work as brothers in rendering service to the human family. For in Christ Jesus this family is called into the family of the sons of God" (*Gaudium et Spes*, 92).

It was a very clear call but what have we done to translate all this into the realms of our own experience? These are the real questions to be faced today. Are we working hard enough to make the family life of our own neighbourhood secure? What about the homeless, the lodgings that are closed to "children and coloureds", the problems of the inadequate members of our community? What support are we bringing to those working for the relief of world hunger, for peace, for the sick and the aged, for alcoholics and drug addicts? Do we merely criticise local government or are we prepared to enter this important field of service to the community? It is in works such as this that we fulfil our duty of proclaiming by example the words and standards of Jesus Christ. But we should not expect a quick response to our efforts. For we preach Christ crucified.

It is interesting to recall the kind of people who responded to the message of the first disciples as they tried to teach the truths of their Master. They were the meek and humble of heart. For the most part they were weak, the sick and the sinful. They were the poor and the downtrodden. They knew the meaning of lack of freedom and how much they needed "new life" to liberate them. When they asked for baptism they did not imagine that it was going to change their circumstances in this life. But they wanted to enter the Kingdom of Jesus Christ to know his love and his grace.

It is often much easier to see things clearly in ages

other than our own. We cannot always see the wood of the cross for the trees of our pet prejudices. These may not be easy times in which to live. There is always the danger that instead of responding to the great challenge of sharing in the renewal of the Church, some people become disgruntled by the new demands now made upon them. We must remember that the means of salvation are the same and that in many ways the opportunities for our sacramental union with Christ are greater than before.

During the Nazi occupation of Holland, a group of Dutch laymen approached a moral theologian for advice as to what they should do: collaborate or resist by subversive activity. His reply was this: "I will not tell you what you should do, but I will tell you who you are". Some may feel that he was dodging the question. Others will agree that he was underlining the real question.

We have to remember that we are Christians and that we have been told to be "his witnesses to the ends of the earth": that Christianity is essentially missionary. When we use these words of the pilgrim Church, we mean that it is not an inward-looking institution, intent merely on preserving and maintaining itself for its own sake. It is a Church existing primarily for others, an outward-looking institution with a missionary task. Its other concerns, no matter how important, are secondary.

The Church is sent as the Son was sent by the Father and as the Spirit was sent by Father and Son. The Son was sent to reconcile and to make at-one: or, as St John puts it, "To gather together in unity the scattered children of God" (Jn 11:52). The Spirit was sent to make other Christs so that "the world may believe" and so that the hearts of men, torn and paralysed by all sorts of divisions, might be touched by the love of God and find in him the power and hope of reaching their full stature as men.

The Christian Church is sent to be a sign of the unity of mankind and the salvation of the world. It follows (to quote a statement from the World Council of Churches) that disunity in the Church "distorts its witness, frustrates its mission and contradicts its own nature". Disunity is a contradiction because it means that the intended sign no longer signifies and no longer effects unity and salvation. Disunity — to quote the Second Vatican Council's Decree on Ecumenism — "openly contradicts the will of Christ, provides a stumbling block to the world, and inflicts damage on the most holy cause of proclaiming the Good News to every creature". To the degree in which the Church is disunited, it loses its power of speaking to the hearts of men, of liberating their energies for the service of God and their fellowmen. Its missionary purpose is obscured.

Unhappily, the very state of Christian belief in the world today has given the impression that ecumenism is motivated by expediency rather than by missionary or evangelical zeal. To some it appears to be a last-ditch stand by the Churches to save something from the wreck caused by secularisation, by the separation of religion from life.

Perhaps we divided Christians need to be humbled in order to listen more attentively to the promptings of the Holy Spirit. But to bring the churches out of separation and isolation into dialogue and cooperation, it is necessary to appreciate clearly the missionary nature of the Church as founded by Christ: to see the relation between the true worship of God and the mission to bring the Good News of salvation to all men.

Our efforts in the cause of Christian unity must include both spiritual ecumenism and missionary ecumenism. As the churches rediscover together the relevance of worship to the life and purpose of those who worship and redis-cover also their true role in the world, Christian people, for all their division, will understand the full extent of their obligations, at home and overseas, and see the impedi-ment of disunity.

HUMILITY IN CHRISTIAN UNITY

There can be few more moving accounts in the gospel than that which tells us how Christ washed the feet of his disciples. The usual ceremony of the Paschal meal had been begun — the meal which Jesus had desired so earnestly to share with them: "I have longed to eat this Passover with you before I suffer" (Lk 12:14). Yet he knew that not all those gathered about him were content. Perhaps some of these very human friends of his were dissatisfied with their places at the supper-table. St Luke tells us that "a dispute arose also between them about which should be reckoned the greatest".

Not for the first time, Jesus decided to teach and correct by personal example. "And he got up from the table, removed his outer garment and, taking a towel, wrapped it round his waist; and he then poured water into a basin and began to wash the disciples' feet and to wipe them with the towel he was wearing" (Jn 13:4, 5).

In days of sandals and dusty feet, this was a service normally rendered by the lowest of servants. It was a menial task which was usually carried out as the guests reclined at their table. Inevitably it was an embarrassing situation when Jesus performed it for the twelve. It was not just the humble nature of the task that humiliated the disciples. It was the utterly unselfish love with which

133

he tended them that brought all their jealousy to an end. Peter managed a short-lived protest, but the lesson was made quite plain by Jesus when he had completed his round and returned to his place at table:

"Do you understand", he said, "what I have done to you? You call me Master and Lord, and rightly; so I am. If I, then, the Lord and Master, have washed your feet, you should wash each other's feet. I have given you an example so that you may copy what I have done to you. No servant is greater than his master, no messenger greater than the man who sent him" (Jn 13:13-16).

These words were spoken with authority and the whole episode gives us a wonderful picture of God's love for us, his poor creatures. The whole of Christ's life is one of love: the very act of Incarnation, when the Son of God took human flesh, is a sign of his love; his passion and death are proof of that love. Yet there is another element, almost an aspect of his love, which is of key importance to our understanding of how we are to be his witnesses, of how we are to try to reflect the love of Christ in our own lives. It is that selflessness which we call humility.

Humility is not really a human quality. It comes from the Creator. The little man who bows in reverence before the great may be acting prudently or obsequiously, but he is not necessarily acting in humility. Truly humble is the great man who bows before a lesser because he recognises in him a mysterious dignity from the very fact of his creation. Humility is not an inferiority-complex. It is voluntary self-abasement. In Christ and in the foot-washing it is overwhelming.

The Incarnation of Christ is the fundamental humility from which all cause of human humility is drawn. Man's very nature finds its dignity in its adoption by Jesus Christ. Humility is not "grand". It is loving, selfless and Christ-like. In the very circumstances of his coming, we see how Jesus was born poor for our sake. In his work with Joseph the carpenter, in his friendship with the fishermen, he chose the simple way of life and the company of those who had to work hard for their livelihood.

In crucifixion Christ chose the most ignominious of deaths dealt out to thieves and murderers. After his resurrection he suffered Thomas to touch the wounds of his risen body; and he lovingly cared for the needs of his disciples by such ordinary hundrum humble service as preparing a meal for them when they should come ashore from fishing. His utterly selfless concern for them must have been uppermost in their minds when, before rising to his Father in heaven, he bade them be "my witnesses to the ends of the earth" (Acts 1:8).

Small wonder, then, that St Paul is urging the Christians at Philippi "to be in the same mind as Christ Jesus", counselled them to be humble and self-effacing. "Each of you", he wrote, "must have the humility to think others better than himself, and study the welfare of others, not his own . . .". Christ dispossessed himself, he reminds them, "and took the condition of a slave and became as men are; and being as all men are, he was humbler yet, even to accepting death, death on a cross" (Phil 2:4-8).

In our following of Jesus there can be no other path: in love, humility and great faith to be his witnesses "to the end of the earth"; sharing in the work of redemption; accepting the role of sacrifice in our endeavour to bring others to the understanding of his truths; steadfast, as were the disciples, in face of criticism and rejection; and waiting with them in joyful hope for that day when he will return to take us to the Father.

In Christ we are invited to share in the work of redeeming the world. Recalling the prayer of him who gave us this mission, the prayer of Christ the night before he died, that we might "all be one that the world might believe", we know that the vocation of all Christians is to live and work in the unity which he won for us by his redemptive death, to live and work in a unity which is a sharing in the life of the Trinity. "You are one body", we are reminded by St Paul, "with a single Spirit; each of you, when he was called, called in the same hope; with the same Lord, the same faith, the same baptism; with the same God, the same Father, all of us, who is above all things, pervades all things, and lives in all things" (Eph 4:4-6).

When we consider our response to this call to be his witnesses, we must honestly admit that the divisions amongst Christians are an obstacle to the belief of many people today. Christ prayed that we might be one, not for our consolation but so that our very unity and unanimity would help others to believe. What is the situation today? If we look overseas, we can recognise how Christian disunity impedes the work of evangelisation, development and even charitable relief. But here at home, the sad truth is that most people no longer care. The breach between religion and "life as it is lived" is so great that our disunity is not so much a scandal as an occasion for cynical amusement. With a divided witness, the hostility with which difficult testimony is received soon becomes indifference. At first such witness annoys, then it is treated with scorn until eventually its credibility is rejected and ignored.

When Jesus washed the feet of his disciples at the Last Supper and prayed for them to the Father, he knew — in spite of all the hardship he had forecast — what was the real danger for them. Only one thing could prevent them from converting the world and that was sin. Only within their union with him could they carry out the task entrusted to them. Sin is an obstacle to that union, and so he prays that they may be holy and united. "Holy Father, keep those you have given me true to your name, so that they may be one like us ... I am not asking you to remove them from the world, but to protect them from the evil one ... Father, may they be one in us, as you are in me and I in you, so that the world may believe it was you who sent me" (Jn 17:11, 15, 21).

The first step to restore the full visible unity of the Christian Church must be the humble attempt of its members to overcome their own sinfulness. Add to this the positive notion of charity and we approach the sign by which we are to be known as the disciples of Christ. "By this love you have for one another, everyone will know that you are my disciples" (Jn 13:35).

Ecumenism is love because mutual love is the necessary way of approach to the disunity which separates us today. Love alone is capable of casting out the fears which arise from lack of trust in one another's motives. Love dissolves the prejudices which often come from our own inadequate loyalties. It illumines the mind to rid us of the bigotry which is so often based on false information about each other's beliefs and practices. It enables our hearts to shed the bitterness left there from the recollection, personal or inherited, of the experience of less happy days. And in all this, our love must find expression in humility.

The basis of this loving approach to Christian unity is our love of Christ himself. The basis of our love of one another is our incorporation into the Body of Christ through baptism. That is why the formal mutual recognition of one another's baptism was such an important step forward. It was the acknowledgement of the bond between us, that we share so much of the life of Christ, including the very mission that he entrusted to his followers. It has, as may be seen from the agreed statements from the Anglican/Roman Catholic International Commission, been a spur to seeking, through theological ecumenism, a more profound understanding of further bonds in belief and practice. It has underlined the opportunities of joint Christian witness in the action we may take together to meet some of the social needs of our times. It has been an encouragement for the spiritual ecumenism achieved through joint Church services, when humbly, lovingly and prayerfully, we place ourselves in the hands of him who prayed that we might all be one.

Despite the happiness of our prayer together we know that we cannot rest in our constant pursuit of a full visible Christian unity. In emphasising our common Christian bond, we cannot ignore the form of Christ's Church here

J

on earth. If we are not honest about this, we are party to a false ecumenism which is the enemy of unity. Our approach to unity cannot be based *solely* on common social action. We cannot ignore doctrinal truth, nor separate from Christ's prayer that "all may be one" the reminder that there must be "one flock and one shepherd".

What came into existence so many years ago as a result of the life, death and resurrection of Christ was a visible community of people, the people of God of the New Testament. As the Decree on Ecumenism says (art. 1): "Almost everyone, though in different ways, longs that there may be one visible Church of God, a Church truly universal and sent forth to the whole world, that the world may be converted to the Gospel".

For this all Christians long, *"though in different ways"*. Prayer together is yet one more proof of a common determination to do God's will, to welcome the breath of his Spirit, who will renew the face of the earth. Our prayers as Christians must be that God may breathe anew his Spirit into all Christian people, that together we may bear witness in one Church to his glory and his salvation, that we may in love and humility show the face of Christ to the world.

ETHICS FOR TODAY

Ethics is said to be a normative science of the conduct of human beings living in societies. It deals with the standards by which the voluntary actions of human beings are judged to be right or wrong. In practice nowadays we often talk of *things* being good or bad: we may make such a judgment of the food and drink we have just consumed or the facilities offered by British Railways. But clearly here we are treating of human voluntary actions, even though we may want to condemn or praise certain things which influence human actions.

For there to be right and wrong there has to be culpability and therefore freedom of will. Where that freedom is diminished, culpability is lessened. Usually someone is responsible for the things which influence others for better or for worse. But I suppose that there are things like tornadoes or earthquakes which the insurance companies call acts of God. I would judge that in some parts of the world the only culpability could be the failure to make adequate preparations against acts of God which experience shows have some frequency of occurrence.

Ethics deals with the "ought" rather than the "is". We can profitably deal with some of the factors by which the Christian determines the "ought" and perhaps take note of why some of the "oughts" seem to be changing for some people. If we recognise that the very fact that many people no longer recognise an "ought" seems to weaken its impact on others, it may help us to take closer stock of our own position. We may even be led — at the risk of a charge of Grundyism — to see the extent to which our urban life and what goes on in Harvey Cox's "secular city" of our own society are in themselves insidiously seductive of our own standards.

Do we remain quite unaffected and untouched by the decline of morals (or liberation from sexual taboos) which is all about us? Are we really better or more mature for the fact that the display of paper-backs on the railway bookstalls no longer surprises us? Is it all water off a duck's back or does the very frequency with which that long-suffering bird is drenched leave it untarnished and us quite unseduced?

Life today is complex and it is no good our pretending that as Christians we possess one large book in which is set out a list of "do's" and "don'ts" dealing explicitly with each new situation or problem with which we are confronted. Some of our troubles have arisen from past tendencies to supply ready-made answers to each new moral question. There are many quite urgent problems today — especially in the medico-moral field — where the full solution is not immediately clear. Often this is because of inadequate knowledge or diagnosis of the situation which we are asked to rule upon.

In particular instances the individual Christian has to make his own responsible judgment. We may say simply that the more his life is modelled on the life of Christ, the more likely he will be to make right judgments in the sight of God. It is no abrogation of responsibility for us to tell someone that he must follow his own conscience provided he takes what steps are in his power to ensure that the conscience may be properly informed of the principles and guidance it needs.

I remember one old lady telling me with a wry smile that conscience was that which felt dreadful when everything else felt fine. That could be an honest assessment. Like every other judgment, the correctness of the dictate of conscience will depend on the information on which it is based and the objectivity with which it is made. It is our duty to follow conscience but it is equally our duty to make sure that conscience has the necessary information to guide us. That is what we mean by an informed conscience. A false conscience will lead us astray.

What information has a Christian to go on when making a conscientious decision? First, the example of Christ, the principles he gave, the life he led. Second, the experience of the Christian community from the time of Christ to the present day. We believe that Christ is with his Church and never ceases to guide and enlighten it. Hence, we add a third source which is the authoritative teaching of the Church.

If I may quote from our Bishops' Statement on Moral Questions: "A conscientious judgment must be conscientiously made taking into account all the guidance which Christ has given us. We must remember that judgment can be warped by ignorance, haste, fear and other factors. In making a decision we are less likely to choose a course that involves difficulty or hardship for ourselves or others. The responsibility for a wrong judgment in such cases would evidently vary. But it must be remembered that Christ told us to expect hardship and even death. He did not tell us to slip away from them. He promised to help us to persevere in spite of them. Circumstances may modify responsibility. They cannot make wrong right or right wrong".

The Second Vatican Council's Pastoral Constitution on the Church in the World Today says that "conscience is the most secret core and sanctuary of a man . . . In the depths of his conscience" — according to article 16 — "man detects a law which he does not impose upon himself, but which holds him to obedience. Always summoning him to love good and avoid evil, the voice of conscience can when necessary speak to his heart more specifically:

141

do this, shun that. For man has in his heart a law written by God. To obey it is the very dignity of man: according to it he will be judged".

There is the Christian picture of conscience, but is it always as easy as that. What in fact *is* the situation? At the present time a large number of people do not regard as wrong or sinful their offences against what *we* judge to be right. They challenge the very validity of our principles. It is one thing to break, say, a commandment and be unrepentant for the sin or offence. It is another to deny the legitimacy of the commandment. Sin has been with us since Eden. What is perhaps new at the present time, at least in extent, is the total rejection of the force of moral law. Sin, as the violation of sacred beliefs and practices, is nothing new. What is qualitatively new is that the very truth and moral validity of so many notions and practices, long cherished in the Western world at least, are being challenged.

I understand that the Americans call it the "hang-loose" ethic. J.L. Simmons and Barry Winograd, in their book *It's Happening*, try briefly to trace the process in their country and to a lesser extent in ours. They claim that Europeans as well as Americans of the past few centuries lived by what they call the Protestant Ethic: a way of life and a view of life stressing the more sombre virtues. It was a kind of positive moderation. Moderation was not just a safe course between extremes. Moderation was an optimum, positive, good in and of itself thing. Moderation was raised almost to a first principle of ethics. It was a mandate on how to conduct your life. It extolled the quiet good feeling of a hard day's work well done, the idea that a good man always more than earned his pay. It was pragmatic but respectable.

This moderation carried over into virtually every aspect of the lives of the people. Even in religion, anything smacking too much of mysticism was suspect. For all the early mystics in this country, we have to admit that overmuch enthusiasm, even speculative theology, was regarded

142

as very un-English. And the same could be said of our moral life. Of course there were bad people but — so it is argued — these were exceptions.

These two American authors argue that with the onset of secularisation in this century the so-called Protestant Ethic gradually changed into what William F. Whyte termed the Social Ethic. Undoubtedly the mushrooming urban areas contributed to this. It was really more accurately the Sociable Ethic, a rather superficial "society and good neighbour" ethic, whereby it was taken for granted that getting ahead was a good thing in itself, with if possible an accumulation of material wealth. It generated a feeling of comfort and goodwill, with a minimisation of risk: almost it became a utopian culmination of the principle of moderation. In Britain we never had it so good. In the States President Eisenhower virtually proclaimed moderation the cornerstone of national policy. Then in the sixties it seemed to slow up. There were new frontiers and a "hip" society. Even before the British Chancellor of the Exchequer decided to let the pound float, the Americans showed us the way by letting the ethic hang-loose.

If the floating pound sank, so the "hang-loose" ethic is in danger of falling right off. The Americans have many helpfully descriptive titles and I suppose that to "hang-loose" was the counter to that restraint which they describe as being "uptight". We must recognise that wherever applied it is basically irreverent. It repudiates, or at least questions, such cornerstones of conventional society as Christianity itself, patriotism ("my country right or wrong"), marriage and pre-marital chastity, civil obedience, the rights of parents at one end and of government at the other to make decisions for others: in fine it rejects the establishment. But it is not just a violation of established institutions in society: it challenges their very legitimacy.

Sometimes that challenge may initially be good. It shakes up complacency. Responsible questioning can often be helpful to a deeper understanding of long-held belief.

Of course it can often lead to aggression and violence. But I think the most important thing about this is not so much the affront to others — parents, politicians, priests, whoever it may be — as the fact that it leads to dropping out and setting up a life independent of conventional society. Some of the social rebelliousness that led to the setting up of communes was at least justifiable and stimulating. But life in the commune, liberated from social and moral laws, has led to lawlessness and sometimes to a mixture of anarchy and phoney mysticism.

The "hang-loose" ethic is not always violent, but with the removal of all restraints there is always the likelihood of a move towards the law of the jungle. In fact one basic aspect of the "hang-loose" ethic is a persuasive humanism which sets great store by at least some aspects of human life — what some people nowadays call the "love-thing", but deprived of the sense of the fatherhood of God which gives meaning to the brotherhood of man.

Another basic aspect of the "hang-loose" ethic is the pursuit of experience as being good in itself, as a means of learning and growing. The idea is that a great variety and depth of experience is beneficial and not at all harmful so long you can handle it. This of course leads to the heightened importance of the present "on-going" moment with less concern for either past or future. It finds expression also in a basic mistrust of dogmas and principles which tend to obscure the so-called richness of life and experience.

No Christian looking for his role in society can today be unaware of the immense paradoxes, if not contradictions, evident in the developments of our age. We remember the Lord's words from the book of Genesis, the instructions given to man by his Creator. "God blessed them, saying to them: 'Be fruitful, multiply, fill the earth and *subdue* it. Be master of it'." Never has the human race enjoyed such an abundance of wealth, resources and economic power. Yet a huge proportion of the world's population is still tormented by hunger and poverty; countless numbers suffer from total illiteracy. The technological achievements in our surroundings serve only to emphasise the poverty which as a result seems even more abject elsewhere.

On the face of it one might imagine that with this new found plenty, those who enjoy its benefits would have an enhanced sense of security, of confidence, even of gratitude to a bountiful Creator who has so richly blessed his creatures. In practice, we know that man, "striving to penetrate farther and farther into the deepest recesses of his own mind, frequently appears more unsure of himself. As he lays bare the laws of society, he seems almost paralysed about the direction to give it" (*Gaudium et Spes*, 4). Thus material development is frequently accompanied by apathetic materialism and by spiritual apathy. It would be false to imagine that "those without" necessarily have a closer relationship with God or a greater sense of dependence upon him. But one can detect that some amongst the new nations, fragile as they are in their developing status, are nonetheless deflected from their goal of stability as much by the imported influences of secularism as by the lingering hatred of their native tribalism.

Where does the Christian stand in all this? When we say that man does not live by bread alone, we mean that he will find no complete satisfaction or peace or prosperity apart from his eternal destiny. The Christian must stand for these eternal values, even when they are a contradiction of what is being said and done by the naturally good humanists who surround him. He must be a figure of hope and faith when, through pressures and failures of so many kinds, those alongside him are affected by depression and deflected from their purpose by uncertainty as to its being worth the candle. He must be a witness to charity when man's natural instinct to self-preservation takes the form of a golden life-jacket bejewelled at least thoughtlessly from the bare necessities of others.

To talk in generalities is relatively easy. When one tries to translate it to reality, inevitably one starts talking about people. The fact is that men were created to live in brotherly communion with one another: fully in eternity, but to a great extent in time also. Though his vision must be of the heavenly kingdom, the Christian here on earth will perhaps play his most significant part in the developments, achievements and changes of today, by reminding himself and others that people are persons, that youth are young persons, geriatrics old persons and that all are his fellow creatures called to fulfil a purpose in the plan of their common Father and Creator.

Someone once remarked to me that when people are no longer treated as human persons, they rapidly become guinea-pigs. I believe that he was thinking of the concentration camps of thirty-five years ago; my mind turned more naturally to geriatric wards, handicapped children, anti-biotics, thalidomide, euthanasia and abortion. It is not so much that there is a danger that we shall hear again in our lifetime of efforts to establish a master-race, as that in our super-powered, cushioned but buffeted age, we may be too busy for those who, despite apparent helplessness, are to the Christian a redemptive element in our company.

As the Christian looks ahead with Christian hope, the expectation of the new Jerusalem, a new heaven and a new earth, must not weaken but rather stimulate his concern for cultivating this earth in which so many of his brethren — and possibly he himself — are floundering. At whatever level of his physical or intellectual capacity, it will always be for the Christian to give witness to this vital appreciation of the dignity of the human individual as he is now.

It goes without saying that for all his limitations the Christian has to try to be like his Master, to go where he would have gone, to do what he would have done. Christ did not surround himself with the successful and if ever the Christian Church were to comprise merely the saints and the successful, let alone just successful saints, I would feel that in some essential way it had lost Christ. When he walked the face of the earth, he moved about amongst the multitude having deep compassion for those who were in sorrow or in need. I believe that in the years immediately ahead this will be a very special role for the Christian.

The sudden shock of Alvin Toffler's "accelerating change" is leaving a great cargo of casualties, physical, mental, psychological, perhaps psychosomatic and certainly moral. I believe that it is the special role of the Christian to share concern for such persons, whether we call them the casualties of our generation or the new poor. I do not believe that to opt out of society is the Christian answer, though I recall the American negro University Professor who told the World Council of Churches that modern society was so corrupt and infectious that the only thing was to get out, organise force in opposition and destroy it. This was my first meeting with Black Power. He asked us to pray that we should have charity and understanding when we found ourselves at opposite ends of a rifle barrel . . . But if we are not ourselves to opt out, we must have compassion on the drop-outs, whose numbers may well increase as Toffler's accelerating change jolts and judders its way to an even greater pace.

Then it will be for the Christian to recall those words from the prophecies of Isaiah which Jesus Christ spoke in the synagogue at Nazareth:

"He has sent me to bring the good news to the poor,
to bind up hearts that are broken;
to proclaim liberty to captives,
freedom to those in prison;
to comfort all those who mourn and to give them
    for ashes a garland:
for mourning robe the oil of gladness,
for despondency praise . . .
For as the earth makes first things grow,
as a garden makes seeds spring up
so will the Lord make both integrity and praise
spring up in the sight of the nations" (Is 61).

And as all eyes in the synagogue were fixed on him, Christ added "This text is being fulfilled today, even as you listen" (Lk 4: 21).

THE PLACE OF SOCIAL SERVICE
IN PASTORAL CARE

So much is heard nowadays about the need for Christians to project an authentic image of Christ that, in considering an approach to almost anything, we have to consider what exactly is the image Christians should be presenting as well as to examine carefully how other people do in fact see us.

We are probably less nervous than we used to be of evangelical expressions like "projecting the image of Christ". Provided we have adequate knowledge of the person, it is always easier to try to copy someone's example, even if in different circumstances, than it is to attempt to portray a theory or give physical expression to an idea.

In October 1974, on the very crisis day of the Synod of Bishops in Rome, when several weeks of work discussing evangelisation seemed threatened and we were almost over-anxious to get to grips with the problem which had suddenly arisen to divide us, we were solemnly invited to leave the Synod Hall and go next door where the Pope had arranged for us to have a preview of an exhibition of contemporary portraits of the person of Christ, as drawn, painted or sculptured throughout the world.

Of course, from every culture and medium the results were very different. Some were almost stark and photographic, some looked like freedom fighters or as if they

149

had walked out of a students' Hall of Residence, some were strictly impressionistic and some, you might say, almost straight from the bush. But it was only after a while that the storms of a divided debate were lifted from our minds and we realised that, where perhaps it was difficult to be precise in a way of general understanding and universal application, the answer to our problems lay in choosing to present in our own lives the image of the Saviour now depicted before us.

We are often told in criticism nowadays that formal and organised — even institutionalised — Christianity bears scant resemblance to the ways lived and taught by Christ. Large numbers of persons who would never dream of darkening the doors of a church will nevertheless turn out in any circumstances to see and listen to Mother Teresa or even to see a film of her work in Calcutta. As we all know, youngsters who have rejected the Church are usually more than willing to endure the ordeal of the sponsored walk to raise money for world development or to go and help clean up and paint the local Old People's Home.

If the followers of Christ are to present his image and follow his ways, there is surely a lesson for us to learn from that papal exhibition of contemporary art. First, the portrayal was seldom if ever exactly the same style or manner of presentation as that which we would recognise as coming from previous centuries. Second, it varied very much in accordance with local culture and was related to settings, customs and needs. You might say that it was indigenous, contemporary and relevant.

These are jargon words but they are not necessarily the worse for that. What we really mean is that living Christianity today must be suited to what is natural (even national) to us; it must be suited to our times and it must be relevant in the sense that it must make sense in the light of our present and actual needs and circumstances.

Indeed, if the Church and its members are to overcome the charge of being a hide-bound formalistic anachronism — all of which ideas hide behind the word "institutional" — then we have to see how its witness and our witness fit the criteria I have mentioned. No one accused Our Lord of being out of date or out of touch, no matter how unpopular the doctrine he preached. It is a charge which we, his followers, cannot sustain without in some way allowing his image to be defaced.

Let us take the briefest look at his public ministry. The gospels make it clear that, with fairly frequent recourse to prayer, Jesus showed his way to the kingdom by preaching, teaching and by going amongst the people, healing and consoling, working miracles and having compassion upon the multitude. He taught by word of mouth and by example: in so doing it was not just what he did but the manner in which he did it which was important.

We cannot read the gospels without seeing that Christ's life was the implementation of the great commandments: the love and service of God, and the love and service of one's neighbour. We can go further. We have to say that the service of those in want is really an essential part of the life and legacy of Christ. For us today it is an integral part of the whole work of evangelisation and of our sharing in the life and mission of the Church.

It is not enough to leave the matter there, either as a general idea or as a theological principle. We have to ask ourselves "Who gives the service?", "To whom is it given?" and "How?". To the first question the answer, at least in theory, must be "all the baptised". Clearly in the context of the pastoral work of the Church such an answer must indicate that the task is capable of communal performance. That does not mean that everyone can leave it to everyone else but that the members of the community must see that the social responsibility of the Church is met, and by each member in accord with opportunity and capacity.

All Christians, from their baptism, share in the life and task of Jesus. Part of that task is the loving care of those in need and so we share that work too. It may mean that our first priority is to provide the wherewithal for

151

the more expert amongst us to get on with the job. But precisely because the needs themselves are so widespread and so local, we cannot feel that we fulfil our responsibilities by the mere payment of rates and taxes.

Clearly such payment is necessary for the social services provided by the State in our name. No one really pretends that, even with the most comprehensive service, every need can be adequately met. We not merely have to try to pick up the pieces which fall through the net-work: we have to remember that we ourselves are part of that wider community which we call the State. We have to play our part in the State's services and in the supplementary voluntary services, especially those operating in our name and in our own area. All this arises from our baptism, and each according to his capacity — physical, financial and job-wise.

To whom do we owe this service? Christ made no distinction and neither can we. We can only answer "all those who are in need and in accordance with the nature and measure of that need". Practically, that can mean in the first place with and through the State's welfare machine and a local authority's Social Services. It means also that we must give responsible support to the valuable work of the voluntary organisations. It means finally that Catholics clearly must support and play their part in the particular responsibilities of the Church of which they are members.

I say "with and through" a local authority Social Services because, although "through" public monies we may contribute to the care of those in need, it is also a case of "with" because we are ourselves part of the larger community. We have to play our role as citizens in the initiatives of those authorities operating in our locality. This applies to the whole Church. Because on the whole this responsibility must be exercised in what are strictly speaking secular surroundings, this work is the special responsibility of those with a primarily secular vocation, i.e. the laity.

The laity are not the only ones whose witness is needed.

There is an obvious case for religious, men and women, e.g. those in the nursing profession, who can bring to the work of the local community the witness of their special dedication. It is not a question of propaganda and flag-waving but of playing our part in the fulfilment of the communal responsibility for those in need.

There can be occasions when such a role has to be carried out by a priest: when there is a particular priestly witness and ministry to be given. Clearly this can apply to chaplains and it can apply also to certain professional spheres where a priestly ministry is of outstanding assistance. In such cases, without being singular to the extent of sticking out like a sore thumb, it is important that the witness and contribution be specific for what it is, and coherent in the eyes and sight of others.

This leads us at once to the question of "how" such service is to be given. Perhaps the most direct, simple and accurate answer is "in a Christ-like manner". If I translate that into "as well as you can", I mean that it must be carried out with all possible competence, as well as in the spirit of loving care, of generosity and humility. The nurse can translate it still further in her own sphere, just as can the hospital voluntary library service, the League of Friends or the ward-cleaners.

We know of course that no state Social Service can nowadays cope with all the needs of the community and this is because there is no uniformity of need and the community is made up of individuals. There may also be special needs in a community due to its make-up: for example, the whole age structure of our island as a community presents special problems in the care of old people. On the continent there are special problems with regard to migrant workers. Equally in many of our towns the failure to achieve what can be called a balanced community can also lead to local stresses and weaknesses which the statutory bodies may not have the flexibility to meet.

Thus it is that the Church, in fulfilling her obligation, has to consider not only how it can encourage its members

K

to act through the State's Social Services but it must also see what additional services it must itself initiate, supply and finance.

If we are to fulfil our responsibilities adequately, there has to be reasonable coordination and even organisation of what we do to relieve the needs of others. By "others", I am not distinguishing them from "our own", as if we had responsibility only for our own people. Certainly we have special responsibility for our own not only because they look to us but also because we even owe it to the whole community that we should play our part. I mention "others" because I believe that apart from personal self-help, I shall as a general rule give a better service and the community as a whole will be better served if what I do fits in with what others are doing.

This is why for the pastoral care exercised by the Church we need our own organisations to advise and sometimes initiate all the works undertaken by the Church and in the name of Christ, whatever the need.

I believe, as I said earlier, that one of the consequences of the speed of change, and its acceleration though at an uneven rate, is that a number of people drop off or drop out of today's society, sometimes from choice but often because they cannot stand the pace at which society is hurtling into the future.

Many of these things must be the concern of the state's Social Services. But the very people who fall off or jump off the machine often make it impossible for that official machine to help them. I believe that the Church and any Catholic Social Service organisations have a special responsibility here. To me the performance of such a difficult and devoted work can be a near-perfect enactment of Christ moving amongst the multitude and having compassion upon them.

RELATIONSHIPS IN MARRIAGE:
OUT OF REVERENCE FOR CHRIST

Some years ago at an international conference on the family I met some very excitable Mexican delegates. I was never able to determine who was a delegate and who was a spouse also in attendance: they were inseparable. The situation was made more difficult by the fact that there was also a blood-relationship between a number of them. But I was a bit shattered when one of the women, with great enthusiasm and love of the Lord, introduced me to a man whom she described as "my brother who is my husband". If she had said "my brother in Christ" it would have helped. Such was her reverence for the bond of baptism and the relationship between the baptised that she was, I suppose, determined to get her priorities right. But at least by the time she introduced me to her brother-in-law I was ready for her.

In Christian marriage the baptismal relationship between the partners is something which must colour the natural and physical bond between man and wife. The epistle to the Ephesians compares marriage with Christ's love for the Church. St Paul tells husbands: "Love your wife, as Christ loved the Church and gave himself up for her, that he might sanctify her, having cleansed her by the washing of water with the word, that he might present the Church to himself in splendour, that she might be holy and without blemish" (Eph 5:25-27). He goes on to say that husbands should cherish their wives as their own bodies, adding: "For no man ever hates his own flesh, but nourishes and cherishes it, as Christ does the Church, because we are members of his body".

Perhaps the key words to remember are "as Christ loves the Church". For we know that this is a total, sacrificial love. He "gave himself up" for love of the Church. In marriage, the husband is the representative of the Lord who, we remember, came "not to be served but to serve" (Mt 20:29). Thus the love of the husband is self-surrender. In his book *The Bible Marriage,* Fr Vollebregt writes of this passage: "Paul describes the relationship of Christ and the Church as a marriage relationship; Christ has won the Church as a bride by his sufferings and death, has cleansed her in the bridal bath of baptism, has contracted a divine marriage with her, and remains affectionately devoted to her".

In the Common Bible translation of Ephesians, we find St Paul advising married people to "be subject to one another out of reverence for Christ" (Eph 5:12). "Reverence" in this translation replaces "fear" or "obedience" more frequently found in other versions. The point about this text is not so much the nature of the fear as that husband and wife have reverence for one another because of their relationship with Christ: because of their membership of the one Body of Christ. Indeed St Paul's constant likening of Christ's relationship with the Church to that of bridegroom and bride not only gives a new dimension to our consideration of marriage: it also shows how as we enter through baptism into the life of Christ, so our attitude to one another must be mutually Christ-like — on both sides of the relationship: and never more than in marriage wherein two members of the Body of Christ become one flesh. The love of husband for wife and of wife for husband has this additional aspect of reverence precisely because that union of flesh is, as it were, in the Body of Christ.

We see the relationship as being sacrificial and sanctifying. We see further that the eternal unity of Christ with his Church is reflected in the one and unbreakable nature of the sacramental bond of marriage. All sacraments imply a bond with Christ's death and resurrection. Marital love is a real token of Christ's love for the Church as he endured all in fidelity upon the cross. That love of the dying Christ upon the cross has called forth undying love from his faithful followers in the Church. So we can say that marriage, founded in love, is a token and sign of the mutual love of Christ and his Church: love which, as St Paul wrote to the Christians in Corinth, "bears all things, believes all things, hopes all things, endures all things, and never ends" (1 Cor 13:7, 8).

"As Christ loved the Church" and "out of reverence for Christ" can have no other meaning. It is the same as when the prophets of the Old Testament compared the Lord's love for Israel with married love. But of course the Incarnation gives new force to such comparisons. Christ's humanity makes the bridal concept more telling. What St Paul is really telling us is not just that the love of Jesus for the Church is like married love: it is really this in reverse. Marriage is like the bond between Christ and the Church, implying unity, sacrifice, redemption: surely the fulness of love.

Striving for these ideals, we realise that God's gifts come to us through Christ and through his sacraments. We recognise that our returns to the Lord are also rendered acceptable in and through Christ: through the merits of his redemption of us. Nothing else really counts. So it was that early Christians, with their great sense of what St Paul called their "life in Christ Jesus", understood that a truly Christian relationship with one another had to be lived in the setting of the Christian community: in what we would have called a Christian atmosphere. The whole of life had to be lived in the expectation of an imminent *parousia* or second coming of the Lord. The Christian community was an enclosed group and this tended to emphasise the communitarian aspect of life and even of marriage itself.

It is as well for us to understand the historical strength of this communitarian setting for marriage. For the truth is that if originally the emphasis was on the community almost as a protective and stabilising element, so over the years it was customarily the community which gave shape and to some extent stability to material relationships.

In centuries gone by and even in fairly primitive society today we recognise what we have come to call the "extended family". It can be tribal or it can be a form of feudalism and squirarchy; but it means that parents, children and grand-parents, cousins and even employees, lived together and almost upon one another and they worked where they lived. The needs of this little community dictated the pattern of the relationships between its members. It was held together by resources gained from its communally-shared work and, even though love was not excluded, the choice of partners in marriage was largely determined by the needs of the community. It was not only among royalty that marriages of convenience were arranged. The perpetuation of that society by child-bearing was of great importance. For very practical reasons the procreation of children held primacy over mutual love.

The structural changes in society in the last century and a half, including industrialisation and urbanisation, have had a profound effect on the shape of society and on the relationships between the families which constitute it. Some of these changes in society have not been to its advantage. But for marriage itself it is at least arguable that the effect of these changes has been no bad thing. Marriage may have been deprived of a number of valuable external supports. These have had to be replaced by mutual love and dependence upon one another: which may well be closer to the sacrificial, sanctifying and saving generosity of Christ's love for his bride and the response of the Church.

Another obvious example of where change has come is in the national social services which have taken over many of the responsibilities previously undertaken by families themselves. One can see a new peak with the anonymity and mobility and lack of relationship in the "secular city" of Harvey Cox. With the general opening up of life, the families have in fact been drawn in more and more upon themselves. The State has taken over many of the functions of the older extended family unit. I personally have a theory that the higher the high-rise building, the less the relationships between those living there. Certainly the truth is that in the urbanised society of today there is less feeling of "belonging", of sharing and therefore of responsibility. Though so much is now the responsibility of the public authority, the individual family often feels alienated from the society in which it lives.

The Americans speak of the "hedgehog syndrome" — of families who just do not want to be involved in the life and responsibilities of their locality. Rejecting the community, at least so far as personal involvement is concerned, the married couple, for whom more is provided, is more drawn in upon its own resources. Place of living and place of work are separated. The very anonymity of their housing separates them from the compelling influences which dictated their parents' marriage in its early years. There is now seldom any fixed social pattern, or, strictly speaking, any objective patterns for better or for worse. How they will live and love becomes a matter of subjective or personal choice. There are criteria, it is true. But, as Schillebeeckx says, "Married couples of today realise that they are faced with the task of building up their marriage into a place of security. This security is no longer given to them when they marry. The task of creating it is something they have to do themselves".

159

The fact that so many women go out to work today means that for almost all couples it is the home and family life which must hold them together — when they get back from work. The old structure of the bread-winner and the queen of the home (or the house-keeper, as the case may be) has largely gone. With women's liberation or the abolition of sex-discrimination, with a realistic equality between the sexes outside the home as well as in it, the old external structural props of formal family relationships and of necessary involvement in the wider society (though a smaller locality) have gone. The very institution of marriage has been challenged. But this has had the effect that marriage now depends, under God, upon the so-called "primary relationships" between the marriage partners themselves. The stability and fidelity of marriage can no longer rely on the extrinsic organisation of society for support. They depend upon the mutual dependence of the couple upon each other.

We may feel inclined at first to bemoan the fact that newly-married couples today have no firm exterior support on which to rely. They have to rely first and foremost on their own relationship, the inter-personal relationship of their married state. To quote Schillebeeckx again: "The patriarchal and authoritarian pattern of family relationships has gone, and a more friendly relationship of companionship and comradeship has taken its place in marriage. Now that the authority of the father in the patriarchal system is no longer necessary even to provide leadership in the family's communal working life, more and more importance is placed upon the existence — between the husband and wife and between the parents and children — of an inner unity and affection, a mutual trust and a close interdependence, whereby each member of the family can find support in the other members when needs arise" (*Marriage: Secular Reality and Saving Mystery*, vol. 1).

Nostalgia inevitably tempts us to count the losses that have come with all these changes. But instead we should try to look at the positive aspects of marriage which present-day circumstances reveal as a living, loving relationship between two individual persons: not just as a convenient "house-able" unit or microcosm of society, but two in one flesh, united in love as Christ is with his bride, the Church. It is a lasting on-going relationship, to be lived day after day, with its "lion-days" and its "mouse-days", as Sam Goldwyn called them. Despite all the pressures from the abuses we have a chance now to see marriage today, stripped of the externals of a mere social contract and shown as a communication and exchange of love between two persons and as an expression of mutual help. We can recognise in marriage an interpersonal relationship which is sustaining, sanctifying and creative, and lived in mutual loving tenderness and consideration "out of reverence for Christ".

I place great emphasis on this constant communication of love because it seems to me to be vital to our understanding of how man and wife must relate to one another as Christ relates to his bride, the Church. But we should be careful lest by using this form of comparison we may seem to exclude Christ's place in the relationship between the couple. *Ubi caritas et amor, ibi Deus est:* where is love and loving-kindness there is God. A loving marriage is a sign of God's presence. Indeed as a life-long relationship it is a sign of his abiding presence. It is this loving presence of Christ in the union of man and wife which makes their marriage a sacrament. It pervades every aspect of their married life. Marriage is not just a matter of being in love but of living love in every aspect of everyday life.

In changed social conditions, when the protective role of society has virtually been withdrawn and the couple must build their married life themselves, this all-pervading love has to embrace not only the marriage-bed, but even the different places where husband and wife may have to work. There is no part-time marriage any more than there is part-time priesthood. They are states of life and are with us all of every day. The husband expresses his love for his wife when he goes to work, just as she expresses her love for him as she carries out the household chores, or just as they both do when they meet together in the evening or give expression to their love for one another when the last child has gone to bed and at last they are alone. A couple's sexual relations are often called "making love together": but all their actions throughout the day can in fact make love.

Perhaps that is the distinction between love and acts of loving-kindness. *Ubi caritas et amor:* where is love and loving-kindness. God is there both times. The acts of loving-kindness contribute to the totality of the love between the pair of them. In relation to Christ St Paul says: "Whatever you do, in word or deed, do everything in the name of the Lord Jesus" (Col 5:3). It must be the same in marriage: whatever is done throughout the day must be done for love of the other partner with whom there is this unbreakable union. It is rather like prayer. We cannot be on our knees all day. Even the Trappist monk, without the distraction of the conversation of others, goes to work in the fields or in the library or even in the wine-cellar, because he cannot be a creature of the spirit all day. St James reminds us that we cannot have faith without works. There are moments for prayer and moments for activity. But if care is taken to thread one's day with prayer, then one's every activity is permeated by the spirit and can become prayerful through our approach to each new task. If care is taken thoughtfully and meaningfully to express love for one's partner — and respond to such an expression of love — then the whole day, however active and whether spent together or apart, can itself be a loving thing.

"As Christ loved the Church" must surely imply this comparison between our communication with God and the communication between man and wife. Is it too much to liken moments of prayer to the sexual relationship between husband and wife? In prayer there are moments when we make the approach and moments when we must listen: and in our demands our love is given in response to his yearning, just as all is done in reverence and respect. "With my body I thee worship" were the words in the old rite of marriage. The tenderness and devotion with which we pray to the Lord, the care we should give to it and the need to ensure that it is not crowded out of our lives through other activities, these are essential elements in our communication with the one on whose love we can always count. There is surely little need for me to elaborate the comparison.

I have used the word "communication" and it will do us no harm to remember that it means "to come into union with". We communicate with the Lord in prayer and often it takes a little while for us to achieve that union or sense of communion of spirit. The effort and patience and love of the preliminaries are no less prayer. So it can be with married love. The preliminaries and care and sensitivity with which the fulness of the expression of love are achieved in the sexual union of the partners are no less love. The very word "intercourse" implies both approach and response. Often the hoped-for loving relationship is endangered by insufficient consideration of the other person. "Christ treats his Church", says St Paul, "as a man looks after his own body. In the same way husbands must love their wives as they love their own bodies". There it is again: "as Christ treats his Church". "And", St Paul adds, "we are its living parts" (Eph 5:28-30).

At the marriage ceremony bride and bridegroom, hand in hand, promise to love and to cherish the other till death do them part. To love and to cherish. Perhaps it is in the word "cherish" that we find best explained the continuing and developing bond of love that must be experienced in marriage. It is not something conferred and it certainly cannot be taken for granted. It is something to be worked on, fostered and always appreciated. The word "cherish" does in fact describe very well how that inter-personal relationship may become Christ-like but only as a result of positive, conscious, continuous effort in action and response. Let the Concise Oxford Dictionary speak for us. It defines "cherish" as "to foster, nurse, keep warm, value, cling to, to hold in one's heart".

The Christian dimension of marriage is surely that the union of man and wife is in Christ and that their relationship reflects the bond between Christ and his bride, the Church. That bond is at the heart of marriage today, seen as the expression of love between two persons rather than as a social contract for the begetting of progeny for the good of society. Again, this loving inter-personal relationship must be nourished and find fruitful communication, just as the bride of Christ (the members of the Church) must take loving care in their communication with their Lord. All this must not be expressed in self-ish separation from the rest of the community. This could scarcely be a reflection of Christ's bond with his Church — established in and for the world community at large.

We are made in the image and likeness of God and surely we can say that marriage is a dimension of the Trinity. Within the Blessed Trinity, the Father and the Son inter-act in a relationship of love. That inter-action we call the Holy Spirit. Within marriage man and wife inter-act in a relationship of love. This, too, is creative in terms of children. Because of the love of Christ dwelling within the bond between the parents, the Christian family which results is itself a sign to others and a leaven within the community at large.

Through Christian marriage Christ speaks to the world of love. Through the Christian family the message of loving sacrifice and redemption is made known to the world. "For greater love no man has than this". In her pamphlet *What is Marriage?* Rosemary Haughton writes: "Christians know clearly that the love they feel for each other, the love which makes them want to live together, is God's call to them to love fully. It is their vocation which they have found in each other".

THE FUTURE OF THE CHRISTIAN FAMILY: AT HOME AND SCHOOL

Many of the present problems in the Church both nationally and internationally reflect those in society as a whole. There are also a number of hopeful signs in the Church and in modern society. One important sign is the present effort of many Christian families to deepen their religious understanding and that of their children in face of the pagan influences so prevalent today.

Parents are well aware of the difficulties and problems of bringing up children in today's world. They know, at least as well as I, the problems of helping their children to achieve real standards of Christian morality and behaviour in the so-called "permissive society" in which we live. There is always the danger of exaggeration. Once a speaker on the subject wrapped up everyday occurences in so many technical terms that the parents amongst his audience said afterwards that they had no idea they had failed to notice so many undesirable tendencies in their children. But dangers outside the home soon penetrate the home itself, especially as children grow up. We all have to be prepared for what may at first seem unthinkable.

Whilst obviously parents have to exercise due care in bringing up their children, it is important to remember that the commandments of God demand both love and trust. They are not just negative prohibitions. To equate Christian morality with caution, let alone fear of being caught, and to present it merely as "Thou shalt not", is to invite from today's adolescents the reply "Why not?"

Obedience to God's laws has to be seen in the setting of love and responsibility. This is not a casual thing to be taken for granted. Life in the home must correspond with what the children are taught. But the parents themselves must adopt a positive attitude to the instruction of their children by word as well as by example. For this the challenges of today mean that many parents must study the problems and the Church's teaching more profoundly for themselves.

Many parents nowadays find it valuable to discuss these matters in groups, with other parents and teachers and, when possible, with one of the local priests present. Here can be a most valuable pooling of ideas, problems and experiences. Where the occasion can include a house Mass all are united in approaching vital questions in the best of all settings. The further extension of the network of house groups and area groups, already established in many dioceses, will be a most important means in strengthening our family life.

Publicity is always given to the question of sex-education of children. This is clearly a matter of concern for those who have at heart the whole upbringing of the child, normally the father and mother. Unfortunately, due to oversensitive reticence or to the fear of being imperfectly equipped for a task over-elaborated with professional mystique, this important responsibility is frequently inadequately carried out by the parents themselves. The onus is then transferred to the teacher who finds it difficult to integrate this matter into his already busy school programme. This difficulty should lead parents and the teachers of their children to discuss this matter together.

Sex is concerned with love, emotions and mutual responsibilities. It is something which children should learn progressively over the years and preferably in the home. Where the children have the joy of seeing the mutual affection of their parents, constantly giving and receiving, the most important element in sexual instruction is assured. The actual facts of physical intimacy, which is also an expression of giving and receiving, may then be made known to the children in the most natural way over the years. Seen against this background, chastity is simply reverence for what is good and lovely in marriage.

All this is only part of the parents' preparation of their children for a mature Christian life. There will always be a period of questioning, about religious as well as moral development. Wise parents will try to share with sympathetic understanding in the doubts and questionings of their growing children. Brash criticism by the young, if accepted with patience, can be a prelude to their more mature understanding of their faith and the values which have inspired the love and trust shown by their parents.

Young people are probably given too much publicity nowadays. To dismiss a whole generation as strong-armed skinheads or promiscuous hippies would be superficial and unjust to the majority. But it would be just as wrong to white-wash wild and selfish behaviour with paternalistic generalisations about the generosity of youth. We have to see beyond strange fads in dress and grooming to the idealism which leads many young people today to reject the self-interest which often governed the lives of some of their elders. The rejection may on occasion be irresponsible and cruel but it can be due to genuine concern for the human rights and dignity of others, whoever and wherever they may be.

Seen in the international focus of our times, where what happens in Africa, Asia or Latin America is through television and press constantly set before us, we must not dismiss the search by young people for the root causes of evil in the world as mere rebellion against law and order. Reactionary measures widen generation gaps. Frustration and repression lead ultimately to a greater explosion. Properly encouraged and given means for responsible expression, this world-wide solidarity of youth can yet become a tremendous force for international peace and justice, without loss to genuine patriotism.

Parents will be able to apply these words to their own family circle, with its differences of outlook and perhaps of interest which can be a cause of tension unless properly understood. Each young person has his own path to tread through life and he may not find it easy to give expression to his ideals. It is the parents' privilege to guide him with loving trust and patient understanding, with a sensible blend of responsible discipline and a ready respect for their child's personal and individual character before God.

Praying together as members of a family can be a great help in this, especially when, within the framework of family prayers, we learn to appreciate the aspirations which lie behind the petitions of the individual. Strained relationships are eased and unasked questions better understood when presented to God for solution in circumstances where the generation gap is levelled through all parties being on their knees. We never grow too old for this.

The lesson of the scriptures is not just a study of bible history. The lesson is now: it is what you do and say now. To teach that lesson is to show people what to say and do now. Since the time of Christ that must surely mean that to teach as a Christian is to try to show others how to live in accordance with the mind of Jesus Christ. This is the task of those who share responsibility for the work of education — parents, Church, teachers and civil society — to collaborate in assisting persons to grow in the fulness of life in Christ.

Because Christ entrusted the continuance of his work to his followers — a task shared by all the baptised — this means that the role of the school in relation to the object of education is to be seen as working with the parents, the Church and civil authority, to achieve for pupils a deeper sharing in the life and mission which Christ gave to his Church. This *is* the fulness of life in Christ. The Church, through parents, priest, Catholic teacher and Catholic school, has the obligation to ensure for its members the help and formation needed for a full Christian life. Ideally, this must mean a full sacramental life, for it is through the sacraments that the meeting with Christ is achieved.

Children must be prepared not just for the reception of the sacraments but for sacramental living: not just for the rite of confirmation but for life as a confirmed Christian: not just for the wedding ceremony but for Christian married life. In the case of confirmation, it is a question of preparing the candidate for the confirmation-based setting in which he is to live his human life, work out his mathematics, learn his French, so that he may fulfil his role in society as a French-speaking mathematician and at the same time may live fully with the the grace and gifts of the Holy Spirit. Bonhoeffer put it more exactly when he said: "To be a Christian is to be fully human according to the mind of Christ".

To achieve this clearly there must be the closest possible collaboration between parents, priest and teacher — between the home or family, the parish and the school. Thus we see that the Catholic school is not just a parish venture deserving support — a desirable appurtenance of a three-star parish along with social club, garage and convent — but a highly important agent of parent, Church and civil society, in helping to achieve the Christian formation of young people for a full life, lived according to the mind of Christ.

This is the fundamental aspect of a teacher's role. In the broadest terms education is preparation for life here and now. Because this relates all facets of life to its main purpose — linking the purpose of life with life-style — then the formation to be given is best presented in a

L

setting and in a spirit and by persons attuned to Christ.

Because we believe — in the words of the Declaration on Religious Freedom — that the "one true religion subsists in the catholic and apostolic Church, to which Jesus Christ committed the duty of spreading it abroad among all men", then for a Catholic child the formation to be human according to the mind of Christ is best presented in a setting, and in a spirit, and by those attuned to the Catholic and apostolic Church.

There really is the case for Catholic schools with Catholic teachers. It is expressed in many different ways, some more theologically rooted, some more practical or pragmatic; in any form it may seem idealistic. But Christianity is really a realistic approach to ideals as well as an ideal approach to the real facts of life. We have to make sure that it is, however, not just mere theory. We have to make sure that it does imply that triple partnership or collaboration of which I have written. Without the collaboration of any one of the three agents or partners the resultant provision is the poorer.

What does all this mean? Take the parents: if they are hopelessly lapsed or living a life in contradiction to the faith being taught to their children in a Catholic school, the best one can say is that the children's preparation for a fully Catholic sacramental life is at least impaired. Take the State: in some parts of the world the political system has led to the suppression of Catholic schools. There again the Church and the parents have to do their best without the help of the school. (The same can be said of those parts of this country where there are not enough Catholic children to warrant a Catholic school). But ask them and they will tell you that it is only second best. Finally take the Church and its role. If the lives of those carrying out its teaching role are in any sense a contradiction of the truths of Jesus Christ, then the acceptability of those truths is at least diminished for the pupil. This applies to both priests and teachers. It is why the apostolic and vocational aspect of the teaching profession has always been stressed by the Church.

In *Teaching the Faith — the new way,* published by the Bishops' Conference of England and Wales, the introduction states: "Catechesis is not only a lesson to be taught, it is also a way of life. In a Catholic school the Word of God which is taught in the religious lesson should be an explicit statement of the principles which are implicit in the life of the school, in the way it is organised and in the relationships of those who work there".

There is scarcely a subject in which in recent years there has not been a radical change in teaching methods and teachers have had professionally to keep abreast of such movement. It is always a cause of concern when Catholic teachers are reluctant to be involved with the teaching of religion "because it has all changed now". Have things really changed so much? Or is it part of a wider reluctance to accept the Church's call to renewal? "All the aspects of the work of the Catholic school are part of the renewal of the Church", it says in that same introduction quoted above. Are teachers and parents really reluctant to take part in the renewal of catechesis and, if so, is it because of reluctance to be involved in change of method or because a deeper commitment to our unchanging faith is called for?

"Every renewal of the Church", the Decree on Ecumenism reminds us once more, "consists essentially in an intensification of fidelity to her own calling". Amidst so much discussion of the reorganisation of our educational system, Catholic teachers are rightly asked to give priority to their consideration of their role in working for the renewal of the Church. In this connection, it is profitable to refer again to *Teaching the Faith — the new way:*

"Our Lord spoke of the scribe learned in the Kingdom of Heaven as a man able to bring out of his treasury, new things and old. In religious education we need to hold fast to two principles: first the stability and continuity which comes from tradition and the Church's magisterium; secondly, a courageous openness

171

and adaptability to the world in which God calls us to live and work. Tradition does not bury God's truth and preserve its bones. Tradition is a living, dynamic developing thing. It never disowns the past nor does it fear the future. Our task of renewal is a difficult one but we must tackle it hopefully. Many years ago, Edmund Campion setting out on a hazardous mission to the England of the first Elizabeth wrote of his own work: 'It is of God, it cannot be withstood' ".

YOUTH AND DISCIPLESHIP

St John, the beloved disciple, writing to the early Christian Church, is straight and to the point. The followers of Christ must be Christ-like. Indeed it is impossible to listen to the gospels and to the writings of the disciples of Christ without realising the inspiration of the Holy Spirit. We realise also the very careful preparation given by Our Lord to those he had chosen to teach his message and to spread what we call, generally, the Christian way of life.

On the face of it the disciples were not a very prepossessing lot: simple honest folk, it is true, strengthened by the professional tax-gatherer, but for the most part fishermen, humble and unpretentious — probably not the ones who would have leapt to our minds if we had been given the task of selecting a team of twelve to spread what were to be revolutionary and vital ideas throughout the entire human race.

We may even be tempted to feel that, as a bunch of supporters, they did not cover themselves with glory when it came to the test: only John was to be found at the foot of the cross; the rest drew back into the crowd, not scoffers exactly but clearly not anxious to show the measure of their commitment. But of course that was before Pentecost. Strengthened with the Holy Spirit there

173

was no holding them, none but was willing to die for the faith of the One they loved so deeply. But apart from this devotion, we must marvel at the manner of their apostolate. We must marvel and we must also draw a lesson from the manner of their preparation for what was clearly a super-human task — to bathe the whole world in the light of the Gospel.

What means did they use? How did Christ himself prepare them? Or to put it in more practical terms, what method of leadership training was employed by the Son of God? The short answer must be "By word and by example". Not only did he lay down the principles but he showed them how to put these principles into practice — even to his death for them on the cross. Never the distant academic teacher, he taught by love and by generous self-sacrifice: the all-powerful God who was born to a virgin in a cave on a hillside: the King of Kings who entered Jerusalem on a donkey: the supreme High Priest who washed the feet of his disciples before giving himself to them at the Last Supper.

Call it service, call it sacrifice: it was overwhelming love, and infinite generosity and dedication. In the end, the disciples understood. They abandoned all personal considerations and with total commitment followed him in life and death. Jesus had taught them to be his witnesses and to share in the saving mission of the Christian Church, of which they were to be the first leaders.

Training for leadership is a matter of prime concern to all organisations, whether these be loose-knit and informal of membership, or more fully-structured, disciplined and uniformed. It has always been true that if you want a man to do a job for you, you try to make sure that he knows how to do it. Nowadays it is given the greatest importance. It may be a case of teaching someone to read the instructions on a do-it-yourself kit. It may be a manual to prepare for a proficiency badge. It may be a university course in agriculture for future farmers. It may be the advanced technical training of a cosmonaut. Or it may be pre-marriage training for an engaged couple. Further education and training are the watch-words of our day.

Yet neither word is adequate: education suggests schools and training suggests physical fitness. Even the word "formation" (used earlier in this book) suggests in English some kind of military tactics or aerobatics. When we reach the combined notion of preparation, education, training, equipping and moulding, we still have to say "Yes, but for what?" For all formation, however broad, must be positively directed to the end in view. If we answer that question by saying "To give effective witness to Christ in this life and hereafter", we see the size of the task of preparing Christian leaders today.

Of course, it is not a question of mere theoretical teaching and listening and learning. It is an elementary principle that formation must be given in practice as well as by instruction, just as it was given by Christ to his disciples. We can add other notions: it must be relevant, suited to our times, professionally competent and founded on faith. But in the formation it is with the manner of the witness, with the character of the leadership required today, and with the manner in which training in that form of Christian leadership is to be given that we must be especially concerned at this time. We cannot overlook the importance of the trainer, the person leading others to leadership. We must live that leadership amongst those we are preparing to be Christian leaders. We must be Christ among men.

I was once present in quick succession at two vast concourses of men and women: one gathering at home and one abroad. They were utterly different places but there were some interesting similarities. Those present were all in some way conscious of human inadequacy, all aware of their personal need, not least the need for inspiration and a sense of direction in their lives. I refer to the so-called "Pop" Festival in the Isle of Wight which I visited, as it was in my diocese, and to a pilgrimage of many hundreds to Lourdes.

Many things have been written and said of the young people who came together in the Isle of Wight and many false impressions have been given. I wish merely to try to draw a limited lesson from this astonishing gathering which combined many aspects of a pre-war Scout Jamboree with a protest march, the last night of the "Proms" and a pilgrimage. Amidst this constantly shifting, seemingly restless, in some manner aimless and yet searching mass of young people, one detected a real acceptance of one another, not just of the sartorial oddities but of needs and weaknesses. This could obviously lead to permissiveness but it could also be the basis of real brotherhood. Lack of discipline in such an atmosphere of acceptance is not the same thing as indiscipline.

If we are to give witness to Christ amongst men, we must accept the challenge of this phenomenon. Christ in his life on earth moved about amongst crowds and had compassion on the multitude. Without being starry-eyed about a situation which is obviously fraught with problems, we must — if we are to exercise real leadership — endeavour to bring a sense of direction and purpose to those who, almost unconsciously desiring what they cannot define, wander in search of each new but passing guru of their generation.

After it was over I had a letter from a young student who had been present throughout the festival. "The thing which impressed me most of all", he wrote, "was the tremendous sense of everyone being together and united. People who had never seen each other before shared everything they had — ground sheets, blankets, food, drink, everything. The feeling was that if you had food and someone else hadn't, then you gave him some. This for me was the most wonderful thing of all". Talk about sharing "pot" if you like, but these words bear a strong resemblance to those used by Christ in training his leaders.

Soon after that experience in the Isle of Wight I went

with a large pilgrimage to Lourdes. There for a week we worked and prayed with hundreds and hundreds of the sick children of God. The incurably sick, the mentally disturbed, spastic children, the deformed and the aged; all turning to their Creator for help and for the grace of acceptance of their role in life. Doctors, nurses, stretcher-bearers, scouts and guides, helpers of every kind, young and old, moving in vast crowds, cheerfully, painfully, searching and praying. Again one had this overwhelming sense of real brotherhood and of the need to be the followers of Christ, Christ moving amongst men, with compassion on the multitude.

It is very doubtful if today's generation will be best served by the dynamic, extrovert, explicit instruction and leadership of the demagogue. Its members would seem to me to need a positive, almost prophetic leadership of presence and witness, sharing, inspiring, listening, counsell-ing, serving, encouraging, loving, living with integrity, teaching by word and by example: but leadership from within, not abstract exhortation and condemnation from without.

Short of extraordinary divine intervention, there can be no short cut by way of instant conversion of a generation: we Christians shall exercise leadership in bringing others to an understanding of our ideals and way of life as we move in humble, uncompromising but compassionate ser-vice among our fellow-men.

As members of the Church, baptised, confirmed Christians, we all share in the mission given us by Christ: young and old, priest and lay, we have the task of living Christ, of bringing Christ to our world. But we are also individuals, with a particular background, special oppor-tunities and problems, and with a specific vocation to answer.

Young and old, we both have an irreplaceable task which no one else can fulfil. But we cannot do it by our-selves: we need each other's backing and we need each other's understanding.

The trouble comes when without adequate knowledge and understanding, different generations talk about each other's worlds and make judgments from their own viewpoint and experience rather than from the realism of the person involved. That does not mean we act in watertight compartments or that we do not try to understand each other's lives. But it does mean that the living Gospel will be brought to the world of young people, whether worker or student, by young people themselves and in their own manner of expression.

To the young people of today the instruction is clear enough: You are the apostles of your own generation, wherever you may be. We used to say "Bring your problems to the Church". I say "Be the Church where you are — but to be so responsibly, share your problems with other members of the Church so that your personal witness may be well-informed and well supported. But you must translate Christ's word to the language of your own day and of your own workshop. Otherwise it will have no meaning to those to whom you are offering it".

SHARING RESPONSIBILITY FOR
MISSIONARY ACTIVITY
IN THEORY AND PRACTICE

About five years after the end of the Second Vatican Council I was in Rome for a plenary session of the Holy See's Laity Council. At the end of our gathering it was announced that Pope Paul would attend a session with us and I was asked to speak to him for a few moments on behalf of the Council about the most pressing needs in the Church at that time. The other members of the Council asked that I should speak about family life and about the world-wide solidarity of young people. But the members from the developing nations of the world asked me to stress the importance of the work of evangelisation. "Holy Father", I pleaded in their name, "the Church needs hope and confidence rooted in the glad tidings of the Gospel. The world needs the Word of God as well as food".

It was at about that time that I began to notice that priests and people, learning to work together, had begun to develop a real sense of the Church. They had, in some measure at least, stopped being parochially-minded and had become conscious of the general needs of their locality, *and* of the world at large. They were realising the size of the Church's mission.

So far as the British Isles were concerned, this was a considerable breakthrough. I recollect that it was also at about that time that I no longer had to reply to questioners who prefaced their remarks by "In this age of the laity . . ." — and whom I would correct by saying "No, in this age of the Church . . .". It was also at that same time that I began to receive letters from priests and parish committees asking for missionary projects to adopt as part of their ordinary parish action.

The work carried out by CAFOD (Catholic Fund for Overseas Development) and Christian Aid is now so much an accepted part of our life that we may forget that to a great extent our first detailed knowledge of world poverty came to us through the mass media. Most information about the sub-human living and dying conditions in parts of India and Latin America came from the colour supplements of the Sunday newspapers and from television and feature programmes. I hope that I shall not be misunderstood or thought to be unfair if I stress this fact and add the comment that in those early days we had scarcely appreciated that this form of relief from poverty and hunger must be regarded as part of the work of evangelisation.

In his letter *Populorum Progressio* Pope Paul emphasised that preaching the Gospel to the poor, the sign of the mission of Christ, includes the work of missionaries to foster the human progress of nations. But so much emphasis has been put on this sort of relief that sometimes there is a danger that missionary activity may nowadays be identified with the work of material relief. This is obviously undesirable in itself but it is particularly important so far as the involvement of the local Church at home is concerned. Certainly many of the relief agencies have emphasised the prayerful and evangelising aspects of relief work. But, as my friends from the Third World had reminded me in Rome, "the world needs the Word of God as well as food".

Missionaries used to wince if the local Church at home

identified "foreign missions" with what many of us called "black babies". Is there perhaps a danger now that we may substitute for black babies Massey-Ferguson tractors, ambulances and Land Rovers? Is the home Catholic to realise his missionary activity by concentrating on his contribution to an irrigation scheme? Did the Good Samaritan also pray for the man in the gutter or merely stop short with bandages?

Again this may seem a little unfair to the missionaries but it is a difficulty which must be faced. I remember talking at that same time to a returned missionary who with great zeal was spending his leave from India preaching Sunday appeals in the parishes. I suggested that it seemed easier to interest people in relief for under-developed countries than it was to engage them in the direct work of evangelisation: that it was easier to secure support for an agricultural school than for a training centre for catechists. I think he must have misunderstood me. "Yes", he replied enthusiastically, "we are always told to concentrate more on material relief than on the administrative expense of sending out missionaries". He then went out to preach to the people: "We do not ask your help for holy water and bibles, but for medicines and foodstuffs". Perhaps he was right: certainly he was carrying out his instructions and so far as the collection was concerned he did extraordinarily well. But, was this, I asked myself, the right approach to people at home wishing to fulfil their responsibility for missionary activity?

It was some time after that particular episode that rather to my surprise I was invited to address a General Chapter of a society for Foreign Missions in this country. I was given as my subject "Involvement of the local Church in foreign missionary activity". I can recall now the four points I chose to make because they had considerable consequences for myself:

"First, please remember that the local Church at home has developed these last years and does not generally require much convincing that it must help with material relief where it is needed. Of course there are exceptions. Generally, however, parishes will do all they are asked in this respect: indeed, nowadays they do not need much asking. Recently, a parish in the south of England, saddled with a huge debt, celebrated the opening of its long-awaited church by a record collection for the victims of an earthquake in Peru.

"Secondly, priests and people long to hear about the work of missionaries, parish priests, nuns and laymen — especially if it is not accompanied by a financial appeal. They will give even more generously the next time. If the parish has planned giving, it will usually be willing to make over part of its annual income in support of missionary activity. This may seem starry-eyed idealism: it could well be the shape of future financial support for missionary activity.

"Thirdly, if a returned missionary visits the schools in this country in the hope of recruiting, he should preach the Church and not the foreign missions. It is important that we see the work as one. Our families must encourage emissaries to come from their number to fulfil the need for priests and religious at home and abroad. Competitive bargaining for vocations is repugnant to the young people who will be generous in giving even themselves when they see that the Church to which they belong must answer wherever the needs are greatest.

"Fourthly and finally, please ask us at home to pray for those to whom the missionary activity is being directed. Recently, a parish priest pleaded in vain with a visiting missionary who had come to appeal to make the whole Sunday a day of prayer, with talks for young people, meetings with parents, and so on. He had been willing if necessary to guarantee a minimum sum as an offering at least as great as the last appeal. His request was rejected in favour of the traditional appeal sermons at all Masses, as this was the mandate provided by the superiors. Please ask yourselves carefully whether this is the best way to involve those at home in the missionary activity of the

Church overseas. Is this the way for the Church of the future"?

To say that my words divided my audience would be an understatement. I·was told that my suggestions were impractical. It was said with some fairness that whilst I tried to work out such missionary theology at home, the missionaries and those to whom they ministered would languish from lack of material support. But the occasion proved a challenge to me as to the missionary society concerned and, although missionary appeals continued, we began to work together to see how it was possible for a diocese on the home mission to be directly associated with the work of a sister-Church in so-called foreign mission territory. With priests and lay people we re-thought a solution as to how we could give effect to the relevant paragraph from the Second Vatican Council's Decree on the Bishops' Pastoral Office in the Church:

"As lawful successors of the apostles and as members of the Episcopal College, bishops should always realise that they are linked one to the other and should show concern for all the Churches. They should be especially concerned about those parts of the world where the Word of God has not yet been proclaimed or where, chiefly because of the small number of priests, the faithful are in danger of departing from the precepts of the Christian life, and even of losing the faith itself. Let bishops, therefore, make every effort to have the faithful actively support and promote works of evangelisation and the apostolate . . . As far as possible, they should also arrange for some of their own priests to go to such missions or dioceses to exercise the sacred ministry permanently or at least for a set period of time" (art. 6).

It was nearly ten years after the end of the Council that, as the hot African sun shone down on a great crowd gathered in Mankon in West Cameroon, I heard those same words incorporated in an address of welcome read to me by the local parish council on behalf of the Cameroonian Diocese of Bamenda.

I was sitting beside the West African Bishop Paul Verdzekov. The words we heard read out clearly rejoiced his heart just as it did my own, because it was such an explicit statement of the understanding which had at last been reached between our two dioceses and which had led to our sending our first two priests from Portsmouth to West Cameroon.

With the help of that same Foreign Missionary Society which I had addressed some years earlier, arrangements had been made whereby our diocese could endeavour to maintain six of our own priests in the Diocese of Bamenda, each serving for a period of six years in all. Some months after the first two priests had settled in, it was suggested that I should go to West Africa myself for a visit to try to assess the situation and see how it might be developed in the future to include religious and laity from the diocese. The visit, in the course of which I travelled many hundreds of miles with the local bishop and with our own priests, was one of the greatest experiences in my life. It taught me that nothing could compare with the Good News brought by missionaries to territories which had not before heard of Jesus Christ. At the same time, precisely because of that Good News, the local people were inspired to endeavour to improve their own situation and that of their brethren.

The local Church was moving steadily forward. The roots had been well laid. But almost everywhere there was evidence of the shortage of technical assistance. This applied to colleges and secondary schools, lacking the help of qualified teachers. It applied also to such things as dispensaries, visited regularly by religious sisters and almost invariably without qualified assistance. Inevitably also the work was restricted by the necessity of the nursing sister having to be responsible also for all the chores of the dispensary.

Before all else one was conscious of the shortage of

priests and here at least was a sphere in which a home diocese could help best of all. Not that there was desire or need to create a "clericalised" Church. In the various out-stations which could only have an occasional Mass from priests ranging over a large territory, there was good evidence of valuable preliminary work in preparation for the liturgy and carried out by the catechists and local teachers.

Wherever I went there was a warm welcome but always the idea of "sharing" rather than of "helping". One evening, at a meeting of a parish council, when we had been discussing how an English diocese could share with Bamenda the Lord's work in Cameroon, one member stood up to say that he welcomed the whole project but just now he felt totally at the receiving end. I replied quite simply that whilst even now we at home would benefit from this collaboration, it seemed not unlikely that in the years ahead Africa would be sending priests to Europe. We must share what we had whilst we had it.

This is not the place to go into details about this particular scheme. The bond between the two dioceses appears to have developed well. The Bishop of Bamenda has visited his brethren in the diocese in England. Further priests have gone to Cameroon even after I ceased personally to be involved in the scheme because the agreement was between the two dioceses, not between the two bishops only. "Twinning" can be a restrictive practice but, since this particular arrangement has been in operation, the support in the diocese for other missionary projects elsewhere in the world has increased not lessened.

I may be allowed this personal reminiscence in that it is perhaps important to show how the theoretical teaching of the Second Vatican Council can be put into effect. If the Second Vatican Council was a watershed in my life, the experience in West Africa ran it very close. Altogether overwhelming is the recollection of the reading at a great Mass which I concelebrated there and when an

M

extract from the first letter of St Peter was read in pidgin English:

"But una be people whe God he done pick 'em; una de work Father-work for King; una be holy country. Them done take una for give honour for God, whe he been nove una for dark, and whe he been bring una for he wonderful light" (1 Pt 2:9).

This one, na God e Talk.

THE COUNCIL AND OUR LADY

When sometimes I hear that our Blessed Lady has been down-graded as a result of efforts at renewal in the Church, I wonder whether people have forgotten that beautiful and final chapter in the supreme document of the Second Vatican Council. I refer to the chapter on the role of the Blessed Virgin Mary, Mother of God, in the mystery of Christ and the Church: the supreme document is of course the Constitution of the Church, *Lumen Gentium*.

There are some who try to justify their argument by saying that this chapter was an after-thought and it might have been expected that the Mother of God would have had a constitution or decree to herself. Yet the decision not to have a separate document and to include the Council's teachings on Mary in its treatment of the Church was quite deliberate: not to down-grade Our Lady but to show her role *in* the Church and devotion to her *in* the Church.

Through the gift and role of divine maternity, Mary is united with her Son, the Redeemer, and with his singular graces and offices. By these, the Blessed Virgin is also intimately united with the Church. As St Ambrose wrote, the Mother of God is a model of the Church in the matter of faith, charity and perfect union with Christ. For in the mystery of the Church, herself rightly called Mother and Virgin, the Blessed Virgin stands out in eminent and singular fashion as an example of both virginity and motherhood.

Virginity and motherhood: two aspects of Mary and the Church which those entrusted to her from the cross so desperately need to understand in the world today. The one symbolising innocence and dedication, the other symbolising love, compassion and care. As the members of the Church try to penetrate society, as they endeavour to bathe the world in the light of the Gospel, these are the virtues of which the Church has supreme need.

Mary's unique role and position have always been recognised in the Church and I believe this is still true. In England, known for centuries as the Dowry of Mary, it is understood that to know Mary is to know Christ, to seek her prayerful help is to have an advocate with the Redeemer himself. It is impossible to think of the Church without thinking of Mary because it is impossible to think of the Incarnation without a mother.

So Mary stands firm with the Church, and the Church with the mother of its founder. When all this was being debated in the second session of the Council, I was sent by the English bishops to explain to the other National Conferences why we were advocating the inclusion of Mary within the treatment of the Church. There was some confusion. One enthusiastic Italian pleaded that the Madonna be honoured *par excellence* and set on her own pinnacle of honour. Begging the question a bit, I answered by asking him whether, when he went to visit the Blessed Sacrament in a church he expected to be able to honour the Mother of Christ in a side-chapel. Or would he have to go outside the building into the street, perhaps into the cemetery? He saw the point.

Mary's place is in the Church. It is important that in our re-orientation and renewal we should lose nothing of our devotion to Christ's mother. We shall not if we understand the relationship between Christ and his Church. Indeed our devotion to the Church of Christ and to Our

Lady in that Church enhances our knowledge and love of Christ and his Gospel. In some ways the best example is the Rosary which some have mistakenly claimed is now "out".

Contrary to what is claimed we are still encouraged to pray the Rosary. This is not just one "Hail Mary" after another. As we pray, we think about events in the life of Jesus and Mary: and also about what these things mean to our own lives today. This adds to our knowledge of the Gospel. It helps us to increase our personal devotion to the Son of God. It should also make us want to imitate his mother whom he shares with us.

That is not as easy as it sounds. Everything we know about Our Lady has to do with the life of Jesus Christ and this seems to lift her example to a height beyond our reach. We are inclined to think of her as the incomparable Virgin of the Christmas card, kneeling serenely in a stable of spotless snow. We should really be thinking of her as a young wife giving birth to her baby in a cave or shed far from her own home. We make her appear so unreal and inhuman that for many people it seems hopeless to try to imitate her.

Virginity and purity — like motherhood — are not always popular virtues nowadays. But in fact the Blessed Virgin Mary did one thing we all have to try to do: to bring Christ into our world. That means we have to teach other people about Jesus and show them by our own lives what it is to be a Christian, no matter how difficult it is for us at times.

It is here that the Rosary can help us. Every priest knows of sick and old people, perhaps near the end of their lives, whose fingers are constantly finding their way round their Rosary beads. It may be a way of their finding strength through thinking of Christ's love for them. It may be their way of asking the help of the one given to them from the cross as their mother. Sometimes it is just a peaceful and consoling way of showing their faith. That is why we placed a Rosary in the hands of Cardinal

Heenan when he died. For Catholics the Rosary is a sign of devotion and total faith, not an obsession with the Virgin alone.

Praying the Rosary can help us all, whatever our age. The only time when we do not say the Rosary is during Mass when we concentrate on the Word of God and the celebration of the Eucharist. Mary always stands aside for her son. But she leads us to him and he left her to us. The Rosary can be an excellent preparation for Mass and thanksgiving afterwards.

By thinking of the Last Supper we understand Christ's love for us. By remembering Mary at the foot of the cross we see what it means to be faithful. By meditating on the resurrection, as we pray the Rosary, we realise that we must be the messengers of the Good News of salvation to a world in great need of hope. By thinking of these things we understand that we must show to the needy the same loving care which Mary gave to Jesus and his apostles.

Mary's place is in the Church, as is that of the apostles and followers of Jesus. May his people today always remember where to find her and seek her intercession in all they have to do: for no one ever sought her help in vain.

WAITING IN JOYFUL HOPE

At the end of the 1974 Synod of Bishops Pope Paul told us: "Keep a healthy optimism and be sustained by a two-fold bold confidence on which, as on two wings, your work must soar towards new conquests for the Gospel: confidence in your labours because you are working for the Church and confidence above all in Christ who is with you, who is living with you, who is making use of your collaboration and experience in order to extend in the world the Kingdom of justice and holiness, love and peace".

No one need pretend that the years of renewal since the end of the Second Vatican Council have been particularly easy. Yet I am one who has been fortunate enough to see much evidence of the joy brought to countless priests and laity through their new understanding and experience of the Church and their share in her mission. There have been times of hopes fulfilled and of outstanding progress, especially in the field of ecumenism. There have been times of strong feelings, of new-found confidence and of disappointment. Yet I believe that even the sorrow which has been involved may well prove to have been part of the purification which is an essential part of any process of renewal.

Not all who began that pilgrim journey in 1965 are still at our side. All too many of those *periti* and Commission-members who worked with me in the night hours during the Council years undermined their health and "have gone before us in the sign of faith". Others in different parts of the world now share with me the burden of the episcopate. Some other few have, in conscience though to my great sadness, even sought their way forward dispensed from the full obligations of priestly ministry. Even though it will have been noted how often in this book I have referred to the Conciliar teaching that "every renewal of the Church consists essentially in an increase of fidelity", we should not presume to judge in individual cases.

It is probably still true that the greatest enemy to renewal is complacency. This stifles the desire to build up the body of Christ. The very state of the world today demands that our Christian faith find dynamic expression in bringing relief, justice and peace to those vast areas of the earth where poverty and violence deface the world of God's creation. All too easily we recall the standards set by Christ in the Beatitudes as if they were a mere scriptural reminder that God's ways are not our ways, and without our fully understanding the Kingdom and our relationship with those whom he has chosen as our fellow-citizens in that Kingdom.

One of the best ways of overcoming such complacency is to try to translate the biblical concepts of two thousand years ago into ideas of our own times. Instead of "happy are the peace-makers", we could have "happy the community-workers in Belfast". Instead of "those who are persecuted in the cause of right", we could have "happy are the Young Christian Workers in prison without trial in a Latin American country for their concern for social justice". To come nearer home, for "happy the gentle", we could say "happy is Sister So-and-so who always manages to put Christ's smile on her tired face when she opens the door for the umpteenth time to the anxious mother, to the parish bore and to the homeless alcoholic on the scrounge". It all becomes a little clearer when we translate the well-known into circumstances within our own experience.

This bore in upon me most forcibly a few years ago when one Sunday evening, during a parish visitation, I was waxing eloquent about the Beatitudes. I was aware that I was not having much success. At one side, in the front pew, a mother struggled to restrain her handicapped child who in his enthusiasm punctuated my every phrase by banging on the bench with the coin given him for the collection. At the other side was a couple I recognised. He was badly stricken, paralysed and often in Lourdes. At regular intervals he let fall from his wheel-chair the hymn books, Mass-sheets and newsletters with which he had been laden. His wife, beside him but exhausted from pushing him to church, had fallen asleep and at least kept the others around her awake with her snoring.

I was in danger of being disconcerted when I suddenly realised that these were the happy ones; these were the blessed of my Father with whom I hoped to spend eternal life. Surely the handicapped child must be numbered amongst the pure in heart: his mother amongst the merciful and the gentle. The stricken man and his wife would be amongst those who mourned or perhaps those who hungered and thirsted after what was right, no matter what the difficulty. Happy were they: their reward would be great in heaven. I had been given a picture of the Kingdom. Could I hope one day to be their fellow-citizen?

One is constantly made aware of the faith and serenity of the "happy ones", the blessed of my Father. It will indeed be a tragic thing if the growing pains of renewal should ever stifle the joy of true Christian living. It is often in suffering that we are able to find that true union with Christ which alone can bring us well-founded joy and faith. The Church has suffered in these last years. Her suffering, like the blood of martyrs, will surely bring the true renewal of the Bride of Christ.

Some months ago I spent a few hours with a group of those who in recent years had, with lawful and valid dispensation, left their priestly ministry. They had come together to pray, now with their wives and children, that they might find their way forward in the life and mission of the Church they still loved and sought to serve. For them especially the way forward can only be one of faith amidst uncertainty. But whilst they prayed for the gift of understanding and tolerance in the Church, my mind turned once more to the better word "compassion". In the shared suffering of compassion there surely lies hope for the renewed Church. By happy accident these men had first met in Advent and had given the name of that season to their group. Advent is above all a time for looking forward, no matter what the past, and of preparation for the second coming of Jesus Christ.

We often call this second coming the end of the world. We are apt to think of destruction and disaster. For us it may seem a day of dread but for the early Christians it was a day of longing. They were eager for the return of their Master and for this visible proof of the triumph of his resurrection. Some of them even stopped work in expectation of his return at any moment. We have gone to the other extreme. To us the whole question of Christ's return often seems so remote that it does not have much impact on how we live our lives day by day.

Of course, if a man thinks of the end of the world merely as a distant nuclear cloud on his horizon, he may prefer to shut his eyes to it and concentrate on present enjoyments. Yet the truth is that in his heart everyone longs for a more perfect life than he has so far experienced. He may be happy for a time but then the moment passes. For a number of reasons his present situation fails to satisfy.

Man's spirit yearns for something more than the present world can give him. "You have made us for yourself, O Lord", wrote St Augustine, "and our hearts are not at rest until they rest in you". Only with the second coming of Christ at the end of the world will all wants and longings be satisfied, our anxieties quietened, our wounds healed and our broken hearts restored to happiness.

St John explains this in the Book of the Apocalypse,

when he tells us of his vision of the end of the world: "God will make his home among men; they shall be his people, and he will be their God. He will wipe all tears from their eyes, there will be no more death, and no more mourning or sadness. The world of the past has gone" (Apoc 21:3-4).

Not surprisingly, the apostles frequently asked Our Lord: "When will all this happen?" Jesus replied in many parables, explaining that the answer was known only to God. "As for that day or hour, nobody knows it, neither the angels of heaven, nor the Son; no one but the Father only" (Mt 24:36). But, although his return would be sudden and unexpected, it need not be a cause of worry to those who were prepared.

Jesus constantly told his followers to be on the alert for the time when they would see the Son of Man returning "in the clouds with great power and glory". In St Mark's gospel he tells us: "Be on your guard. Stay awake, because you never know when the time will come" (Mk 13:33). But the day of his coming is a day of fear only for the sinner, the person who ignores the teaching of the gospel. If we follow Christ with fidelity and charity, we are ready and prepared.

We have somehow to rediscover the approach of the early Christians who lived in constant hope of Christ's coming. For them belief was strengthened by love. They longed for his return because they loved him so much as a person. Our longing for his second coming will not be real unless we too have a deep love for the person of Christ.

Our Christian life must be a constant commitment to our Master, the Jesus whom we know and love in our prayer and whom we meet in the sacraments of the Church. Our love for him should make us long for his coming, so that we can be with him. The prayer of the early Christians, "Come, Lord Jesus", needs to be the prayer of Christians in our own day.

Great consolation may surely be gained from the beautiful words, now prayed by the priest at Mass after he has said the Our Father: "Protect us from all anxieties as we wait in joyful hope for the coming of our Saviour Jesus Christ". All the other desires and recommendations contained in these pages pale into insignificance beside these words. We have to rediscover a living hope and joy at the prospect of the Lord's coming again: that day of glory and triumph in which those who have been faithful will share.

"For if we continue to love one another and to join in praising the Most Holy Trinity — all of us who are sons of God and form one family in Christ — we will be faithful to the deepest vocation of the Church and will share in a foretaste of the liturgy of perfect glory. At the hour when Christ will appear, when the glorious resurrection of the dead will occur, the glory of God will light up the heavenly city, and the Lamb will be its lamp (cf. Apoc 21:24). Then the whole Church of the saints in the supreme happiness of charity will adore God and 'the Lamb who was slain' (Apoc 5:12), proclaiming with one voice: 'To him who sits upon the throne and to the Lamb be blessing and honour and glory and might for ever and ever'" (*Lumen Gentium*, 51).

Remembering my words in the Introduction to this book, let me end by saying quite simply: that is what the Church is all about.

GIVE ME YOUR HAND